W9-BNO-612

Jazz
Dance
Class

Gus Giordano

Jazz
Dance
Class

Beginning thru Advanced

A Dance Horizons Book
Princeton Book Company, Publishers

JAZZ DANCE CLASS: BEGINNING THRU ADVANCED.
Copyright © 1992 by Princeton Book Company, Publishers. No portion of this book may
be reproduced in any form or by any means
without written permission of the publisher.

A Dance Horizons Book
Princeton Book Company, Publishers
P.O. Box 831
Hightstown, NJ 08520

Cover design by Anne O'Donnell
Interior design based on the design used in
Anthology of American Jazz Dance (Chicago,
IL: Orion Publishing House, 1978).

**Library of Congress Cataloging-in-
Publication Data**

Giordano, Gus.
    Jazz dance class : beginning thru
advanced / Gus Giordano.
        p.   cm.
    Summary: Uses the format of a jazz
dance class to introduce specific exercises, anatomical information, and standard jazz dance terminology.
    ISBN 0-87127-182-6
    1. Jazz dance—Juvenile literature. [1.
Jazz dance.] I. Title.
GV17484.G56   1992
793.3—dc20   92-22623
Printed in Canada

Contents

Introduction

≡

Jazz dancing has had a long and colorful evolution. Consider the many, varied dance forms that have fed into jazz, making it such a rich dance medium: African dance, ballet, modern dance, show dance, theater dance, social dance, and East Indian folk movement. Jazz has always been a reflection of the trends and temper of the times. Early in America's history, jazz music and dance had their foundations in the culture of African slaves. It wasn't until the 1920s, "The Jazz Age," that the population at large started to admire and emulate the contribution of black musicians and dancers. In the 1990s, music video dancers, club dancers, and street dancers have sparked a new interest in jazz, especially among young people. Today, jazz dance is universally recognized as a uniquely American contribution to dance art.

Acknowledging the distinction between the established vocabulary of jazz dance and its newer, popular manifestations, this book has been written for dancers and teachers who want a foundation in the basic principles.

Jazz dance as an art form is the perfect blend of mind and body founded on a firm technical base. Therefore, it is beneficial that students come to jazz with some training in ballet or modern dance. Classical training not only gives the student basic vocabulary, but it also teaches discipline in the legs and feet. Discipline is as inescapable in jazz as it is in any other dance form. Flexibility, center placement, clean lines, multiple turns, leaps, and the ability to quickly transmit combinations from the brain to the body are the nuts-and-bolts of technique. The student seeking a career in dance learns very quickly, by failure at auditions, how important technique is

HOW TO USE THIS BOOK

Jazz dance celebrates sensuality. Its character is not romantic, like ballet, nor is it highly reflective, like modern dance. Therefore, jazz requires a mature body, and it is preferred that jazz training not begin until the onset of puberty. Foremost, the student must view the body as a personal instrument, as a keyboard with infinite possibilities. With this in mind, students should be groomed and dressed in a way that allows the teacher to observe all nuances in movement. Isolation moves, turns, and flexibility of the feet are all lost in bulky clothing and footwear.

The jazz classes presented here are prefaced by a list of standard terms and a brief overview of human anatomy as it relates to dance movement. These sections were written with the beginning student in mind, and can either be presented in their entirety, early in the course, or they can be broken down and discussed throughout the course, at the beginning or end of class.

Classes are presented for beginning, intermediate, and advanced students. At each level the class begins with primary stretches that focus on breathing, isolations, floor stretches, and pliés. This section of class along with floor stretches and barre stretches should be done bare-footed so that the student can feel the power of the floor. The next stage of class involves jazz walks that coordinate the isolated movements of the head, the rib-cage, the pelvis, and the feet. The student ceases to move in an isolated manner and works the actions into a fabric of dance. From this point onward, students should wear jazz shoes.

Along with the primary stretches, there is a list of finger positions and exercises that is also applicable to each grade level. It is extremely important that choreography be created for the entire body, even in floor exercises. The fingers and hands are most often neglected, so I have described finger movements that are commonly used in jazz dancing. These are my invention in the sense that I am the first to attempt to codify jazz finger movements. Because of their novelty, they should be practiced regularly until they become a natural part of the student's vocabulary.

A large portion of Grade I class is devoted to stretching, conditioning, emphasizing proper placement, and technique. In the beginning, relatively little class time is spent on combinations. As the class progresses, and students become more familiar with the basic stretches, isolations, and walks, more focus and time can be shifted to combinations. Beginning jazz combinations should be kept simple, with the stress on clean technique and repetitions. Remember to start slowly then progress to faster tempo.

With Grade II begins the demarcation of jazz styles: afro-primitive, lyric, modern, musical-comedy, and rock. Turns, hops, jumps, and leaps are also introduced here. With these additions, proper placement, especially of the knee, is of the utmost importance to prevent injury. By this stage of instruction, students are spending more time moving across the floor and are primarily focusing upon coordinating isolation moves.

Grade III increases the complexity of combinations and emphasizes the further development of technique and style. At this level, the primary stretch is augmented by a pre-stretch that consists mostly of isolations. This helps prepare students for the more rigorous demands of this class. Another notable addition to this level is the jazz barre. Knowledge of classical ballet technique is necessary for the jazz barre, and it is not appropriate for beginning students. Finally, the advanced class will probably take longer than either the beginning or intermediate classes, so plan accordingly. If you are limited by time constrictions, you may want to alternate sections of the lesson every other class.

Jazz dance has been my life's work and a constant joy. I hope this book will help lead students and teachers alike to feel the same exhilaration as I do—whether in class or in performance.

Gus Giordano

Standard Terminology

All Fours

FACE TO FLOOR

FACE TO CEILING

Arabesque

Attitude

FRONT—TURNED OUT

FRONT, TURNED IN

BACK, TURNED OUT

BACK, TURNED IN

SECOND, TURNED OUT

SECOND, TURNED IN

Back Bend

BACK

POSITION 3

Battement

Body Roll

FORWARD

POSITION 4

POSITION 1

SECOND

POSITION 2

POSITION 5

Chest Lift

TOP OF HEAD

Contract

POSITION 1

POSITION 2

POSITION 3

Coupe

Crossed Swastika

Feet Positions

FIRST POSITION PARALLEL
(Neutral)

FIRST POSITION,
TURNED-OUT

SECOND POSITION PARALLEL

SECOND POSITION,
TURNED-OUT

Feet Positions—Continued

FOURTH POSITION PARALLEL

FOURTH POSITION,
TURNED-OUT

FIFTH POSITION PARALLEL

FIFTH POSITION,
TURNED-OUT

Fetal Position

KNEES

SIDE

BACK

Frog Position

Head Positions

1—NEUTRAL

2—DIAGONAL

Head Positions—Continued

3—PROFILE

4—SIDE TILT

5—RELEASE

6—CONTRACT

Head Positions, Adding Arms

1—V POSITION FRONT

2—V POSITION OVERHEAD

3—INVERTED LONG JAZZ ARM

4—HEEL PRESS

5—INVERTED LONG JAZZ ARM

6—LONG JAZZ ARM

Hip Lift

LOW

HIGH

Inverted Long Jazz Arm

Inverted V Position

Jazz Hand

Knee Hinge

45°

FLOOR

Knee Position

NEUTRAL

TURNED-OUT

TURNED-IN

Lay Outs

FORWARD—LEG 2nd

SIDE

FORWARD—LEG BACK

Long Jazz Arm

Passe

NEUTRAL

TURNED-OUT

TURNED-IN

Pelvis Position

SIDE

RELEASE

CONTRACT

Perch

Pique

Plie

DEMI-PLIE

GRANDE-PLIE

"PLIE-RELEVE" POSITION

Release

HEAD, RIB-CAGE, PELVIS

Releve

Rib Cage Positions

SIDE

RELEASE (FWD)

Rib-Cage Positions—Continued

CONTRACT (BK)

**Second Position
Leg Stretch**

Shoulder Stand

Side Stretch

Sous-Sus

Splits

SIDE

FORWARD

JAZZ

Square

FORWARD

SIDE

**Stretoh for
Lengthening Back**

FORWARD

SIDE

Swastika

OPEN
SITTING

LAY-OUT

Tabletop

TORSO

LEGS

V POSITION

BACK

Tendu

Torso Twist

FRONT

LAY-OUT

V Position

OVERHEAD

FORWARD

DOWN

Anatomy

HEAD

The placement of the head influences the general control and stability of the body. The head, a first-class lever, can move like a see-saw, controlling the center of gravity. The most prominent focal point for the dancer is the lifted regal-looking head on a long neck. The neck (or cervical area of the spine) gives the head more freedom than any other part of the body.

The head is the heaviest part of the body for its size, consequently neck muscles and tendons must be stretched regularly in order to remain strong for the unique isolated manner in which the head moves in jazz and rock. The head is the signature for the jazz style.

Attitudes of the Head

Neutral Position
Diagonal
Profile
Side Tilt
Release (Back)
Contract (Forward)

Types of Movement

THRUST—Sharp, percussive movement, forward or back.

VERTICAL—Lifting up and down movement, like saying "yes."

HORIZONTAL—Swinging side to side movement, like saying "no."

LATERAL—Tilting movement, side to side, fare remains front.

ORIENTAL—Thrust movement or circling in any direction.

HALF HEAD SWING—Semi-circular movement, left to right or right to left.

HEAD CIRCLE—Full rotation of head right or left.

The popping noise that is heard when doing neck and head movements is the calcium deposits being dispersed, allowing for greater freedom in this area.

SHOULDERS

The shoulder isolation is the look of jazz. This isolated movement gives the arm that punctuated feeling of strength. The isolated shoulder has become synonymous with the look of jazz dance.

Beginning movements of the arm are initiated in the shoulder area, the arm held in place by the shoulder girdle. The ligaments are loosely wrapped around the shoulder joint, thereby giving a great amount of flexibility to the shoulder region.

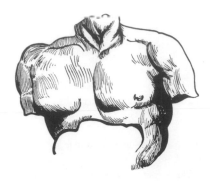

Isolation Movement Positions for the Shoulder

Neutral
Up–Down
Forward–Back

Half Rotation Forward
Half Rotation Back
Full Rotation Forward
Full Rotation Back
Push–Pull

ARMS

Movement of the arm begins in the shoulder joint and the shoulder girdle.

Port de bras is the movement of the arm in isolated sections.

The objective of port de bras exercise is the freedom of movement of the arm through discipline.

In order to achieve this, the muscles and tendons in the arm are used in an oppositional manner which constitutes a counterforce, such as movement with muscles and ligaments tightened, used to achieve the pressing style of jazz arms.

Breakdown of the Arm into Its Moving Parts

Hand
Wrist
Elbow

Shoulder
Fingers

HANDS AND WRIST

The hand and wrist owe their unusual mobility to their generous supply of joints.

No piece of modern machinery is more delicately constructed or more perfectly coordinated than the human hand.

Strong finger action requires a rigid wrist, but

the most powerful wrist action can only take place if the fingers are relaxed.

Positions

LONG JAZZ ARM—Continuous line from the shoulder to the fingertips with elbow lifted and slightly pulled back. Fingers are held together and palms are parallel to the floor (usually done in second position).

V POSITION—Open line from the fingertips, through the arm (armpits open), across the chest, through the other arm and to the fingertips. Placement may be down, forward of chest, or overhead.

INVERTED LONG JAZZ ARM—Continuous line from the shoulder to the fingertips with elbow slightly dropped, with fingers held together and palms up (usually in second position).

JAZZ HAND—Palm forward with open extension of the fingers from thumb to little finger; wrist must be rigid and straight.

PORT DE BRAS—Carriage of the arms through various positions.

Types of Movement

THRUST—Quick, accented movement with percussive beat.

SUSTAINED—Slow, connected movement with a lyrical rhythm.

SWING—Suspended, rhythmic movement

that oscillates back and forth, giving a flowing, connected movement to the arm.

CIRCULAR—Quick (percussive) or slow (lyrical) movement of the wrist, shoulder, elbow or the entire arm. Circles are made into or away from the body.

PARALLEL—Both arms moving from center of body to overhead, or down to sides with elbows bent and back of the hand front, forearms remain parallel (also used diagonally).

ROCK—For the most part sharp, percussive movements accompanied by the funky movement of the released rib-cage and pelvis.

Breakdown of Movement

Jazz Hand
Fist
Long Stretched Fingers: fingers are together and thumb follows line of fingers
Wrist Leads
Wrist Circles
Fan: Fingers are clenched and open individually starting with thumb, ending with little finger. Fingers fan and open away from body.

TORSO

The torso is the trunk of the body and houses the shoulders, rib-cage, spine, abdomen and pelvis. Movement, in order to be organic, must begin in the abdominal area and send electric waves out through the head, the fingers, and the feet. If movement does not begin in the center of the torso, it looks and feels mechanical. The emotional zone is expressed through the upper part of the torso.

Diaphragm breathing, open at the top and closed at the bottom, with the rib-cage opening and closing like an accordion, gives the torso a living, pulsing quality.

The torso is the control center for all appendages' movements.

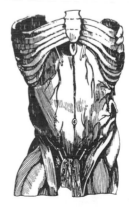

TORSO PLACEMENT

Square or Neutral Position

The spine is a vertical line from skull to tailbone. Pelvis and shoulder girdle are horizontal lines. Rib-cage top open, bottom closed. Counter stretch between rib-cage and pelvis. Abdominal muscles tight. Pelvis is tilted forward, spine is pulled to its longest and strongest line.

Rib-Cage Positions

NEUTRAL or SOUARE.

RELEASE—Thrust forward.

CONTRACT—Concave position back.

RIGHT AND LEFT ISOLATION—Lift and place right or left.

Pelvis Positions

(These are covered in the following section.)

Bending Positions

TABLETOP—Bending forward from hip-socket, vertebrae straight, face addressing floor, stomach muscles tight, arms V position overhead.

BACK BEND—Spine bending back, face parallel to ceiling. Arms second position, inverted long jazz arm.

SIDE STRETCHES RIGHT AND LEFT—Abdominal muscles tight, arms V position overhead, shoulders down.

TORSO TWIST—Face profile right or left and twist ribcage and shoulder girdle forward, arms fourth position. Pelvis remains in profile position.

PELVIS AND HIP

The pelvis serves as the container for the hip socket. For best possible amount of flexibility in the hip socket, keep the pelvis fixed. Ligaments that hold the hip joint to the pelvis are strong and very tough (the hip joint is more securely put together than the shoulder joint). These ligaments must be stretched daily to keep the hip joint at maximum flexibility.

Breakdown into Placement Areas

Neutral or Square position

Release (Back)

Contract (Forward)

Side Right and Left

Diagonals Right and Left

Circles Right and Left

Square:
Contract to Neutral
Right Side to Neutral
Release to Neutral
Left Side to Neutral
(This square also reverses.)

SPINE

Mankind's real Achilles heel is his back, and the only way to a healthy back is through exercise.

Our spines are arranged in a beautiful way—knit and woven into a very pliable column by very strong and elastic ligaments.

Leaning forward will build up the muscles of your back; swings from side to side build the side back. Leaning backward will build the abdominal muscles.

The abdominal muscles and the back work together as a team. If stomach muscles are weak they will not give proper support to the spine and the back may become strained and painful.

The area of the torso that houses the abdominal muscles and small of the back is called the Magic Area: stomach muscles firm, back straight and lengthened, and the rib-cage lifted high off the pelvis creating a cavity in the center of the torso.

Breakdown of the Spine

The spinal column, arranged like 33 building blocks with one vertebra piled on top of another, are held together by ligaments; and there are cushions between the vertebrae to hold them apart.

The skull, rib-cage and pelvis are all attached to the spine and are moved separately in an isolated manner. The spine is smallest at the top (skull) and bottom (pelvis) and largest at the small of the back. If the small of the back becomes weak and too curved, the top and bottom of the spine are consequently threatened.

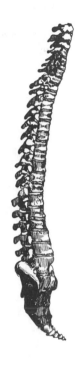

Positions

Neutral Position
Release (Forward)
Contract (Back)
Side Right
Side Left
Diagonal Right
Diagonal Left
Circle Right and Left

LEGS

Dancing is a locomotor skill, self-propelled mainly by the use of the legs. Consequently, the greater power of the leg drive, the greater the acceleration and energy of the dancer. Efficiency in dancing requires the elimination of all unnecessary force, so leg movements must be quick, accurate and precise.

The ligaments, tendons and muscles of the leg must be thoroughly warmed up in order that there will be no internal muscular resistance.

Economy of effort is a highly desirable objective; the problem of overcoming inertia de-

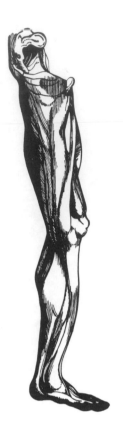

creases if the legs have reached a totally warmed state.

Because of the legs, the dancer has that period of no support—the "sailing through air" quality.

Breakdown of Parts

Thigh
Knee
Hamstring
Shin
Calf
Ankle
Foot

FEET

The foot has two dance functions of tremendous importance: support and propulsion. It is usually described as an elastic arched structure.

The foot requires great strength and firm support since its function is to carry the weight of the entire body. The toes, especially the large and powerful "big toe" are largely responsible for propulsion; they provide the push-off movement.

Strength and elasticity of the foot are due in large measure to ligaments which bind the bones together. The foot should be used with almost as much flexibility as the hand. Circulation of blood through the body improves with greater movement of the feet.

Movements of the Feet

POINT—Stretched, arched instep, toes pointed.

FLEX—Bend at ankle.

CIRCLE—Rotate ankles right and left.

UP, DOWN—See-saw movement.

RELEVE—Toes and metatarsal (round bones at base of toes) grip the floor, lift heels high (done from plié position).

PLIE—Toes and heels gripping the floor, controlled bending at ankle and knee.

HALF-TOE—Stepping out on the toes and metatarsal (knee locked) without the preceding plié (called pique in ballet).

PLIE-RELEVE POSITION—Toes and metatarsals grip the floor, heels lifted high, knees flexed.

Breakdown of Foot

Toes, metatarsal, ball, instep, arch, heel, achilles tendon, and ankle.

BREATHING

Start any dance class or any class that requires stretching of muscles, ligaments and tendons with a breathing exercise in order to begin with fresh oxygen. Oxygen feeds the blood, blood feeds the muscles.

Never hold your breath while stretching. If you have breathing problems, you need better abdominal muscles. Anyone who lives a very quiet life has breathing problems. If you take daily walks, shout or do a lot of laughing, you abdominals will be fairly strong, and will become stronger through exercise.

A progressive breathing exercise to take the old oxygen out of the body and give a new, fresh supply:

SITTING ON FLOOR   LEGS SEMI-YOGA
                   POSITION
ANKLES CROSSED   HANDS AT KNEES

1-4   Inhale through nose, balloon the stomach

1-4   Exhale through mouth, making a hissing sound—deflate stomach

1-4   Inhale as above

1-8   Exhale as above

1-4   Inhale

1-16 Exhale

1-4   Inhale

1-24 Exhale

1-4   Inhale

1-32 Exhale

1-4   Inhale

1-40 Exhale

The longer the sustaining of hissing out the oxygen, the more you pull stale oxygen from the lower diaphragm. *Don't panic!* In order to endure to the end, you must be relaxed (as if you were filled with sand and it is spilling out over the floor as you exhale). At the end of the breathing exercise, try 3 spurt hisses to insure getting all the oxygen out of the diaphragm.

Isolation Breathing Exercise

LYING ON FLOOR WITH PALMS
ON FLOOR NEAR PELVIS
1. **Using Stomach Muscles**
   Inhale 4 counts, balloon stomach, exhale 4 counts. Deflate the abdominals. (You cannot get oxygen into your stomach; you are using the abdominal muscles in order to strengthen them and to place the oxygen low in the diaphragm. This type of breathing is done for greater energy.)

2. **Using Rib-Cage**
   Inhale 4 counts, open the rib-cage, exhale 4 counts. Close the bottom of the rib-cage. Abdominal muscles are not used in this exercise; they remain firm and tight throughout. The rib-cage opens sideways (like an accordian). This is breathing for dancers, as they cannot use their stomach muscles in an open, relaxed placement or they would lose their center strength. And a relaxed stomach doesn't look very attractive in a leotard.

   When the bottom of the rib-cage is closed, hold 4 counts with stomach flat, small of the back into the floor, rib-cage separated as high as possible from pelvis, and shoulders down.

THE DANCER'S CENTER

Vertebrae lengthened.

Maximum separation between rib-cage and pelvis.

Rib-cage open at top, closed at bottom.

Abdominal muscles tight, as if you were wearing a wide belt at the waist of the torso to keep you pulled in, controlled and lifted.

Shoulder girdle and pelvis maintain a horizontal line.

Shoulders remain down and relaxed with shoulder blades open.

Pelvis is tucked under.

Neck is long and head is carried high and exalted.

The dancer's center is the area from which movement originates and the place from which the dancer works. If this center (or sometimes called square) is maintained, the dancer will be in control of efficient bodily motion with the absence of unnecessary or wasted movements. The result is smoothness and grace and well-coordinated energy and force.

"The dancer's center is an important characteristic of skillful performance, since waste movements and unnecessary tensions not only make for awkward performance, but also hasten the onset of fatigue and increase its intensity."

Kinesiology—K. F. Wells, Ph.D.

Dictionary

A TERRE: On the ground.

ADAGE: A combination of slow, controlled movements.

ALL FOURS: Hands and knees on floor, back flat, face to floor, or hands and feet on floor, torso flat, face to ceiling.

ALL-OVER STRETCHES: Time savers, exercises that do the whole body all at once (body roll, jogging, sit-ups, push-ups, side, forward and back torso stretches)

ALLEGRO: Lively, brisk movements and music.

ARABESQUE: The body is supported on one leg, feet may be turned out or not turned out; the knee may be flexed or locked. The other leg is fully extended to the back.

ARABESQUE PENCHEE: The body slants forward, while back leg is extended in arabesque position. Torso can be arched or in lay-out position. Supporting leg may be locked or in plie.

ARM SWING: A movement of the arm. Arm swings across body from shoulder or swings to second position, or swings overhead. Elbow flexed or locked.

ATTITUDE: The body is supported on one leg. Feet may be turned out or not turned out, the knee is flexed or locked. The other leg is lifted in back or forward with the knee flexed (the attitude may be turned out or not turned out. There is also an attitude in second position turned out.

BARRE: A term used in the dance studio for preliminary warm-up exercises. Exercises are done at a horizontal bar. Exercises are also done standing center floor without using the bar for balance.

BARREL TURN: A turn on one foot, arms extended to second position. Example: right turn—start fourth position, right foot back, on half toe; turn right on left foot. Arms start first position; during turn arms swing to second position. Head spots forward looking over left, then right shoulder. Right foot does passe back to front. Supporting leg is flexed or locked.

BARREL LEAP TURN: A leap turn in the air; head spots forward, arms in second position. Example: right leap turn—cross right foot over left in plie, step left foot in place, leap onto right foot making a full turn in the air. Knees are flexed during turn. Finish leap landing on right foot, then left foot, and stepping right foot forward. Arms remain extended from shoulder throughout. Head spots forward looking over left, then right shoulder.

BATTEMENT: A movement in which the working leg is lifted from the hip into the air and returned to the floor. The working knee is locked, supporting leg may be flexed or locked. Foot flexed or pointed. Move of the battement may be done forward, second, and to the rear.

BODY ROLL: A rolling movement (grande-plie position) that starts at the knees and continues moving through the thighs, pelvis, rib-cage, head and arms (a released open position of the body). May end in a back lay-out or upright standing position.

CATCH STEP: Two steps taken in any direction using one and one-half counts of music.

CHEST LIFT: The chest releases and lifts to its uppermost forward position. The rib-cage expands by inhaling through the nose with the mouth closed. Chest returns by contracting rib-cage (rounding upper part of vertebrae). Exhale air by opening mouth and pushing air from lungs.

CHAINE (turns): Fast two step turns that take two steps to complete one turn. May be done releve, demi-plie, or grande-plie.

COMPASS TURN: A turn on one foot, other leg extended to second position. Supporting leg may be flexed or locked; extended leg is locked and toe is pointed. The turn is executed with the extended leg making full circle on the floor. Arms are usually in second position, but may be placed in any direction.

CONTRACTION: To reduce or become reduced in size by drawing together. This movement applies to the parts of the body that are linked together by the vertebrae, as the head, rib-cage and pelvis. Contraction exercises add to the production of movement.

CORKSCREW TURN: A descending or ascending turn. Starts with legs crossed, and after reaching up or down position legs are crossed again. If turning right (XLOR), if turning left (XROL). (Spiral)

CORNER AND SIDE DIRECTIONS:
C—Corner S—Side
AUDIENCE
(Downstage)

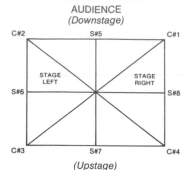

(Upstage)

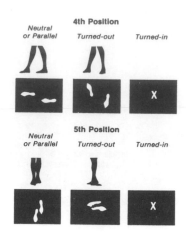

COUPE: One foot cuts the other away and takes its place. A sharp cutting exchange movement of the feet. May be executed in the air or on the floor.

DEGAGE: Point of the foot with fully arched instep. Lift foot off floor.

DEMI-PLIE: A half bending of the knees, also called flexing of the knees. Feet may be turned out or not turned out. Knees extend over toes.

EN CROIS: Shape of a cross. Exercise or movement may be executed fourth position front, second position or fourth position back.

EN DEDANS: Circling into the body.

EN DEHORS: Circling away from the body.

EN L'AIR: In the air.

FEET:

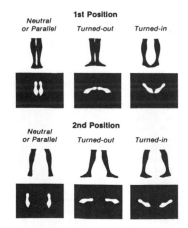

FLEXED POSITION: A bent position.

FOUETTE: Quick whipping movement—moving from one direction to another, sharply. May be performed on the floor or in the air.

FRAPPE: Strong striking movement, brushing the ball of the foot on the floor and into a strong point and arched foot a few inches off the floor.

FROG POSITION: Sitting on the buttocks, with knees in second position, feet together (legs form a diamond shape). Heels are usually off the floor, but may be on the floor depending on the movement. When heels are on the floor, the foot is in sickle position.

FUNKY: A rock movement, with the pelvis, ribcage and head in a released position. Used with all types of foot work and turns. Accent up on the beat; pile "and" count before the beat.

GLISSADE: A gliding step, moving in any direction, with the other foot closing to the gliding foot.

GRANDE-PLIE: Deep knee bend. Heels lift off the floor in first, fourth or fifth position. Heels remain on the floor for second position. Legs may be turned out or neutral.

HALF TOE: A step taken directly on the ball of the foot; heel is high and knee is locked. Press big toe and round bone (metatarsal bone) under big toe into floor, keeping all toes on floor (called "pique" in ballet).

HIP LIFT: A lift of the hip in any direction, forward, side or back.

HOP: Taking off and landing on the same foot.

HITCH KICK: A scissor kick involving both legs kicking in the same direction. Movement may be done forward or back, knees locked and toes pointed.

INVERTED LONG JAZZ ARM: Palms up, fingers together, arms stretched in second position, elbows parallel to floor and slightly flexed.

ISOLATION: A movement separating one part of the body from other parts of the body, i.e., taking a part of the body and placing it out of its normal position.

JAZZ HAND: Palm of hand facing forward with fingers stretched.

JAZZ SISSONNE: A leap into the air starting and ending with feet together. Preparatory plie, leap into air, legs open in opposite directions. Forward leg locked, back leg flexed. Finish landing on forward foot; close back foot forward. Sissonne may be done right or left, forward or back. Arms may extend to any direction. (End of sissonne may be done landing with foot turned out or not turned out.)

JAZZ SPLIT: A slide to the floor ending with forward leg locked and back leg flexed. Right toe slides to C#1 knee locked, right hand extended to floor, left arm extended overhead. Back leg is flexed and turned out. Right hand reaches floor in order to break fall. Split is done to either side.

JAZZ SQUARE: Take four steps making a square on floor. Cross right over left; step left foot back, step right foot second, step left foot forward.

JAZZ WALK: Walks done in demi-plie position, no turn out, feet in parallel position. Rib-cage is released, head high. Feeling is that of a lifted head and torso pulling in opposition to legs in plie position.

JETE: A leap from one leg to another. Working leg is brushed through the air, forward, other leg is extended back. Leap is done forward, back, or to the side. Leap may also be done with back leg in attitude position.

JUMP: Taking off and landing on both feet.

KNEE HINGE: A position of the torso in which heels are lifted, knees flexed, and body is a straight line from knees to top of head. Pelvis must remain locked. Knee hinge may be done in demi-plie, grande-plie, or knees touching floor. (Feet and knees must remain in parallel position for hinges.)

KNEE ROLL: A circling of the knees. The knee roll is done with feet in second position, no turn out. Knees may roll to right or left, in demi-plie or grande-plie position. Knees and feet must remain in parallel position, no turn out. Do not roll over on ankles.

KNEE SLIDE: A floor slide done on knees with body in knee hinge position. Arms placed in any direction.

KNEE TURN: A turn done on both knees, using right and left knee separately to complete full turn. Body remains parallel to walls. Pelvis must remain under rib-cage; do not release or contract pelvis. As you turn, feet lift upward.

LAY-OUT: A straight line position (parts connected to vertebrae in a line—head, rib-cage, and pelvis). May be forward, back or side.

LEAP: Taking off with one foot and landing on the other foot. Also taking off from both feet and landing on one foot.

LEAP TURN: A two-step turn and jete. Step through with back foot and repeat. These are done in a series on one side, then reversed to the other side. Arms are placed in various positions. May be done on diagonal or in a circle.

LEG SWING: A swinging movement of the leg with the knee in flexed position. Direction of the leg swing may be forward, back, across, second, inward circle, or outward circle. Arms usually hold in second position.

LIGAMENTS: Connective tissue with the greatest amount of elasticity.

LOCKED POSITION: A tightening of parts of the body in order that they remain in place.

LONG JAZZ ARM: Arms stretched to second position, strength to and shooting out of fingertips, palms down, fingers and thumb together. Slight flex at elbows, elbows parallel to back wall, muscular part of arm to ceiling.

LYRIC: Movement that flows and moves smoothly from one phrase to the next. (See SUSTAINED.)

MUSCLES: A band or mass of contractile (having the power of shortening or enlarging) tissue in the body that affects bodily movement.

OUTSIDE TURN: A turn on one foot. If turning right, the left leg is the supporting leg; if turning left, the right leg is the supporting leg. Other leg is at passe position, no turn out; supporting leg is flexed or locked.

PARALLEL POSITION: Lines of the body not meeting or intersecting.

PAS DE BOURREE: A series of three steps (can be on half toe or in plie). Steps may be taken in any direction.

PASSE: A movement of the leg and foot in which the position of the leg changes from front to back or to second position. Foot may be pointed or flexed.

PELVIS LIFT: A lift of the pelvis in any direction—forward, side or back.

PELVIS ROLL: A circling movement of the pelvis, usually forward, side, back, side. May be done right or left. Feet and legs are in parallel position, no turn out. Knees are flexed.

PENDULUM SWING: An arm swing movement from the shoulder with the elbow flexed, the hand higher than the elbow. A finger snap may be added to this movement.

PERCUSSIVE: Strong, striking movements which create a heavy accent to specific counts of the music.

PIQUE: (See HALF TOE.)

PIROUETTE: A spinning turn done on one foot. Supporting leg is locked or flexed. Turn is done in place.

PLIE: To bend the knees. Also called a flex position. Demi-plie is a half bending of the knees. Grande-plie is a full bending of the knees. (In French, any bend of the body is plié.)

"PLIE-RELEVE" POSITION: An important jazz position in which the knees are flexed, the heels are lifted high. Control from thighs.

PORT DE BRAS: The carriage, placement and movement of the arms.

PRANCE: A hopping motion. Hop to one foot while the other leg is extended forward (attitude). Knee in flexed position, toe pointed, turned out. Reverse to other side. Arms in second position. Rhythm: 4 fast prances and 2 slow.

PROMENADE: Pivot turn, lift heel, and pivot on ball of foot. Working leg may be in any position. Supporting leg is usually locked.

RELEASE: To disengage or become elongated in size by stretching parts of the body to an extension other than normal.

RELEVE: A lifting of the heels. Knees locked or flexed. Feet may be turned out or not turned out.

RENVERSE: Body bend during a turn.

ROND DE JAMBE: A circular movement of the leg—circles into or away from the body.

SAUTE: Any movement where feet leave the floor.

SCOOP: A movement in a curved line convex downward (moving forward or back). Usually applies to head and rib-cage in order to straighten the back. Movement also applies to arms.

SEAT SPIN: A turn sitting on the buttocks, knees usually in flexed position, and toes resting lightly on floor. Hand is used as pusher.

SIDE JAZZ WALK: A walk stepping to second position with torso facing forward. Feet not turned out, knees demi-plie, parallel position. As step is made to side, hip isolates to opposite side. Arms placed in any position.

STAG LEAP: Stag position denotes lifting front foot to knee of back leg, during leap. Back leg may be in attitude position, turned out or not turned out, or back leg may be in arabesque position.

Torso is lifted facing forward, or parallel to floor. Arms are placed in various positions

SOUS-SUS: Releve in fifth position, moves forward, back or side. (Looks like one foot.)

SPIRAL: Circular movement of the torso, done in any direction.

SPIRAL TURN: A winding turn. Body may begin at standing position and lower to the floor, and may return to normal position. Turn may be done on one foot, or by crossing one leg over the other. Arms are usually placed in second position (corkscrew).

SUNDARI: Oriental head movements.

SUSTAINED: Elongated movement, moving slowly with sustained transitions from one movement to another.

SWASTIKA POSITION: Sitting on floor with one leg flexed in forward position and the other leg flexed in back position. Both hips must be placed evenly on floor.

SWASTIKA SPIN: Sitting on floor, swastika position. It is a turn on the buttocks, starting in swastika position. Pull knees into chest, toes touching floor lightly when turning. End turn in swastika position on opposite side. When turning right, use right hand to push on floor; when turning left, use left hand for the floor push.

TABLETOP POSITION: A movement bending from the hips, with pelvis, head and back in one continuous straight line. Legs are in flexed or locked position. Tabletop position is more difficult when the knees are flexed.

TENDONS: Hard bundle of fibers by which a muscle is attached to the bone.

TENDU: Foot glides forward, second or back without lifting toe off floor. Lift heel and instep as high as possible without lifting toe from floor.

THREE-STEP TURN (Side): A full turn requiring 3 steps to complete the turn. First step is taken to the side, second step is taken making ½ turn facing back, third step is taken making ½ turn facing front. Head spots side, back, front—three steps turn, then reverses to other side. Arms in first position, but they can be placed in various positions. Also may be done forward and back.

THRUST: A sharp accented movement of any part of the body. A sudden impulse usually associated with isolated movements that attack and withdraw quickly.

TOMBE: A fall; body falls forward, back or side onto working leg in plie.

TORSO TWIST: Pelvis facing one direction—holding, while rib-cage, shoulders and head twist to another direction. Example: if pelvis is facing side, rib-cage, shoulders and head twist to the front.

TOUR: Turn of the body (TOUR EN L'AIR, turn in the air).

TRIPLE: Any time three steps are taken to two counts of music. Directions may be forward, back, side or turning. They are walking or running steps. Triples in specific directions are also called chasse, pas de bourre, step-ball change, or triplet.

TWO-STEP TURN: A full turn requiring two steps to complete the circle. Turn may be done with locked knees, plie-releve position, or on flat feet with flexed knees. Arms are placed in various positions. Head spots line of direction of the turn.

TURNED IN: A position which usually applied to feet, knees, or hip. When these parts of the body are turned in, the torso from the waist up remains parallel to front. A turned in movement usually has the knees in a flexed position.

TURNED OUT: A position where feet, knees, and hip are turned so they are facing on a diagonal line. A turned out position may have the knees in a locked or flexed position.

V POSITION SIT: Sitting on buttocks, legs off floor, extending to ceiling. Knees are locked, toes pointed, arms in V position overhead. Back is straight with torso in square position.

Abbreviations

AB—At Barre
ARAB—Arabesque
ARD—Around
AST—At Same Time
ATT—Attitude
B & A—Bow & Arrow
BD—Bend
BK—Back
BKWDS—Backwards
BR—Body Roll
C#1—Corner #1
C#2—Corner #2
C#3—Corner #3
C#4—Corner #4
CB—Center Barre
CHK—Check
CON—Contract
CT—Count
CTR—Center
CTS—Counts
DEV—Developpe
DIAG—Diagonal
DOTL—Double Outside Turn L
DOTR—Double Outside Turn R
DS—Downstage
DWN—Down
ELB(S)—Elbow(s)
ETC—Etcetera
EXD(S)—Extend(s)
FA—Forced Arch
FLR—Floor
FP—Frog Position
FRT—Front
FT—Foot or Feet
FWD—Forward
GP—Grande Plié
HD—Head
HND(S)—Hand(s)

ILJA—Inverted Long Jazz Arm
ISOL—Isolation
ITL—Inside Turn Left
ITR—Inside Turn Right
JH—Jazz Hand
L—Left
LJA—Long Jazz Arm
LOB—Lying On Back
LOD—Line Of Direction
LOF—Lying On Floor
LOR—Left Over Right
LOS—Lying On Stomach
NEUT—Neutral
NTO—No Turn Out
OPP—Opposite
OSWT—Open Swastika
OTL—Outside Turn Left
OTR—Outside Turn Right
OVHD—Overhead
PDB—Pas De Bourree
PDBras—Port De Bras
POS—Position
PP—Parallel Position
P/R—Plié-Rélevè
PT—Point
R—Right
RC—Rib-Cage
RDJ—Ronde De Jambe
REL—Release
RELS—Release
REV—Reverse
ROL—Right over Left
RPT—Repeat
S#5—Side #5
S#6—Side #6
S#7—Side #7
S#8—Side #8
SHL(S)—Shoulder(s)

SL—Stage Left
SLOL—Side Layout Left
SLOR—Side Layout Right
SOF—Sitting On Floor
SR—Stage Right
SS—Sous-Sus
STR—Straight
TBTP—Tabletop
TI—Turned-in
TO—Turned-out
TOG—Together
TT—Torso Twist

US—Upstage
VPS—V Position Sit
WP—Wrist Press
X'd—Crossed
X'g—Crossing
X's—Times
XLBR—Cross Left Back of Right
XLOR—Cross Left Over Right
XRBL—Cross Right Back of Left
XSWT—Crossed Swastika
XLOR—Cross Left Over Right
XROL—Cross Right Over Left

Warm-up

Primary Stretches

Preparation for Class:
Small Towel
Waist Elastic
Band Aids
Deodorant
Leg, Foot and Torso Warmers
Stirrup Tights and Jazz Pants
Leotard
Jazz Shoes
Knee Pads
Hair Tied Back

Shoes and jazz pants are not worn
during the first part of class.
(Stretches are done in bare feet
and tights.)

Primary Stretches

Note: *Used for all grades*

RIB-CAGE AND STOMACH ISOLATIONS (incorporate breathing)

LOF   Knees & FT flexed   HNDS on rib-cage

COUNTS	BODY MOVEMENT	ARMS
1-2 (Sl. Ct.)	**Expand rib-cage—inhale thru nose**	**HNDS at bottom of rib-cage**
3-4	**Close bottom of rib-cage— exhale thru mouth**	
1-4	**RPT above 4 CTS**	
1-2	**Release stomach—inhale**	**HNDS on stomach**
3-4	**Contract stomach—exhale**	
1-4	**RPT above 4 CTS**	
1-2	**Expand rib-cage**	**HNDS on rib-cage**
3-4	**Close rib-cage**	
5-6	**Release stomach**	
7-8	**CON stomach**	
1-4	**Hold above POS**	
1-36	**RPTabove 12 CTS 3 Xs**	

HEAD ISOLATIONS

LOF   Arms beside torso
Legs STR   Toes PTD

COUNTS	BODY MOVEMENT	ARMS
1-2	**Lift HD face parallel to ceiling (neutral POS) Palms on FLR at pelvis**	
3-4	**CON HD FWD**	
5-6	**Neutral POS**	
7-8	**Release HD BK**	
1-2	**Neutral POS**	
3-4	**Turn HD R**	
5-6	**Neutral**	
7-8	**Turn HD L**	
1-2	**Neutral**	
3-4	**Hold Neutral POS**	
5-8	**Return HD to FLR**	
1-24	**RPT above**	
1	**HD Neutral**	
2	**CON HD**	
3	**REL HD**	
4	**HD Neutral**	
5	**HD R**	
6	**HD L**	
7	**HD Neutral**	
8	**HD DWN**	

NEUTRAL HEAD POSITION

ARCH AND LIFT CHEST
TO TOP OF HEAD

LOF   Arms 2nd POS
Palms DWN   Legs STR   Toes PTD

COUNTS	BODY MOVEMENT
1-4	**REL BK to top of HD**
5-6	**Expand rib cage**
7-8	**Close rib cage**
1-4	**Return to shoulders**
5-8	**CON BK into FLR**
1-48	**RPT 3 CTS**

Progress this exercise by placing elbows on FLR at waist
with HNDS P.P. in air. Next progression—clasp HNDS
to ceiling and RPT chest lift as above.

CHEST LIFT TO
TOP OF HEAD

ARCH TO SQUARE

LOF   Arms 2nd POS   Palms DWN
Legs STR   Toes PTD

COUNTS	BODY MOVEMENT	ARMS
1-4	**REL BK to sitting POS (called square)** **(Keep BK arched until square)**	**Use HNDS for support as you lift torso**
5-8	**Pulse torso FWD over legs. BK STR**	**Reach past FT — V POS**
1-2	**Scoop torso FWD over legs**	**V POS OVRHD**
3-4	**Sit square**	**Press 2nd POS**
5-8	**CON to FLR**	**Jazz HND LJA**
1-48	**RPT 3 Xs**	

CHEST LIFT —
HEAD LIFTING OFF FLOOR

SQUARE POSITION SIT

LEGS UP & OVER

LOF   Arms 2nd POS or OVRHD on FLR

COUNTS	BODY MOVEMENT	ARMS
1-4	**Lift legs to 90° knees locked**	**OVRHD — V POS on FLR**
5-8	**Lift FT OVRHD to FLR**	
1-8	**Turn toes under and pulse TWD BK wall**	
1-12	**Slowly lower BK to FLR, legs 90°**	
1-16	**Flex and PT FT as legs return to FLR**	
1-44	**RPT above**	

Exercise also done with interlaced
fingers at nape of neck.

UP AND OVER

NEUTRAL PULSE — HIP SOCKET FLEXIBILTY

LOF   Arms 2nd POS   Palms DWN
Legs STR   Toes PTD

COUNTS	BODY MOVEMENT	ARMS
1-2	Lift R leg	2nd POS
3-4	Pull R knee to tabletop POS	HNDS on knee
1-8	Pulse R knee to chest 8 X's (Neutral)	
1-8	Pulse R knee turned out	Press knee with R HND
		Pull ankle with L HND
1-8	RPT Neutral pulse	
1-8	Pulse R knee turned in	Press knee with L,
	Diminish to 4 pulses	pull ankle with R
	(Neutral—turned out; Neutral—turned in)	
1-16	RPT the pulses in each direction.	
	Diminish to 2 pulses	
1-8	RPT the pulses 2 X's in each direction.	
	Diminish to 1 pulse	
1-16	Pulse 1 X in each direction 4 Xs	
1-8	Pull R knee to Forehead	Arms wrap under R knee
1-8	Hold knee to forehead	Open arms to 2nd POS LJA
1-4	Develope R leg to ceiling	2nd POS LJA
5-8	Return body and leg to FLR	2nd POS on FLR
1-100	Reverse & RPT all to L	

NEUTRAL PULSE

TURNED-OUT PULSE

TURNED-IN PULSE

KNEE TO FOREHEAD

"Move rhythmically."

STRETCH FOR FORWARD BATTEMENT — Slow

LOF   Arms 2nd POS   Palms DWN   Knees locked   Toes PTD

COUNTS	BODY MOVEMENT	ARMS
1-4	Slow Grand Battement R leg to 90°	Interlace fingers BK of calf or ankle
1-16	Slow pulse — stretching leg FWD. (This is the warmup.)	
1-8	No pulse — hold position. This builds the stretch.	
1-16	Slow pulse — flex ankle. (Stretch for BK of leg)	
1-8	Hold	
1-48	RPT all above (remember leg on FLR, knee locked, toes PTD).	
1-100	Reverse & RPT L	

STRETCH FOR
FORWARD BATTEMENT

FORWARD BATTEMENT—Fast

LOF   Fast Grand Battement

COUNTS	BODY MOVEMENT	ARMS
1-2	Knees locked and toes PTD. Lift R leg and return to FLR. 4 Xs R, 4 Xs L. Exercise also done with flexed foot.	Arms in 2nd POS, palms DWN
1-8	RPT using L leg	
1-16	RPT R & L legs.	

BATTEMENT LEG SWINGS—LOF

May be done lying on back & lying on side

COUNTS	BODY MOVEMENT
1	Battement R leg 2nd POS — PT toes
2	1st POS
3	Battement leg FWD
4	1st POS
5-8	RPT above 4 CTS
1-8	RPT L
1-16	RPT R & L
	Also done with flexed foot. Also done with both legs AST.

BATTEMENT 2ND POSITION

LEG LIFT FOR STRENGTHENING THIGH MUSCLES

SOF   Legs in 1st POS   Toes PTD
Palms on FLR next to knees   BK STR, bending FWD

COUNTS	BODY MOVEMENT
1-2	Lift R leg from hips (6″ off FLR) — Point
3-4	RET to FLR
5-6	Lift L leg 6″ off FLR
7-8	RET to FLR
1-8	REV & RPT L leg
1-8	RPT using both legs
	(Also done with flexed feet.)

BATTEMENT WITH
PALMS ON FLOOR

OPEN-SWASTIKA HIP ISOLATION

SOF   Swastika POS (R leg FRT, L BK)
Arms 2nd POS LJA

COUNTS	BODY MOVEMENT	ARMS
1-2	Contract & isolate L hip FWD (off FLR)	
3-4	Return R hip to FLR by releasing Hip	
5-8	RPT	
1-4	Torso lies BK	Place elbows and palms on FLR, BK of hips
1-8	Contract and isolate L hip FWD & return	
1-4	Place BK on FLR—torso square POS	2nd POS, palms DWN
1-8	Contract and isolate L hip FWD & return	
1-4	Extend R leg to C#1	
1-8	Contract and isolate L hip FWD & return	
1-4	Bend R knee & lift torso to R	L arm circles above HD
5-8	Change Swastika to L side	
1-48	REV all L	

CONTRACTED HIP—
SWASTIKA POSITION

CROSSED SWASTIKA ISOLATION

SOF   R FT across L knee
Bend L under FWD   Sit on both hips

COUNTS	BODY MOVEMENT	ARMS
1-2	CON R hip FWD	2nd POS LJA
3-4	ISOL rib cage L	2nd facing S#6
5-6	Torso twist L	
7-8	Turn HD L	
1-2	REL R hip to FLR	
3-4	Return rib cage to Neutral	
5-6	Hold	Return arms facing FRT, 2nd POS
7-8	Return HD to FRT	
1-16	RPT above 16 CTS	
1-2	Develope R 2nd	
3-4	Develope L 2nd	
5-6	Fold R in front	
7-8	Cross L over R (ready for L side)	
1-32	REV L	

CROSSED SWASTIKA POSITION

SWASTIKA ROLL AROUND

SOF   R leg FWD (bent at knee, R toe at L knee,
L knee bent BK, L toe BK of Body Torso Square,
Arms 2nd POS   LJA

COUNTS	BODY MOVEMENT	ARMS
1-4	Sit in above POS. Bend to R side.	Place R palm on FLR at R side, L arm circles OVRHD
5-8	End with shoulders on FLR	Arms 2nd POS
1-4	Lift torso to SOF POS	Place R palm on FLR. L swings OVRHD
5-8	Sit in square POS	Arms 2nd POS LJA
1-24	RPT 3 Xs	
1-8	PT L to 2nd (off FLR). PT R to 2nd. Place L leg FRT, R leg BK (2 CTS each movement) (Now you are ready for L side.)	Same
1-32	RPT on L side	

SWASTIKA POSITION
SHOULDERS ON FLOOR

SWASTIKA POSITION

ARCH TO BACK BEND

LOB   FT parallel   2nd on FLR
HNDS wrapped around ankles

COUNTS	BODY MOVEMENT	ARMS
1-4	Arch to SHL	**HNDS hold ankles during entire first part of stretch.**
1-8	Pulse TWD BK wall	
1-4	CON to FLR	
1-4	Arch to SHL	
5-8	Arch to top of HD	
1-4	Hold 4 CTS	
5-8	CON to FLR	
1-4	Arch to SHL	
5-8	Arch to top of HD	
1-16	Place HNDS by ears on FLR and lift into backbend. Hold.	BACK BEND STRETCH
1-4	RET to top of HD	
5-8	RET to SHL	
1-8	RET to FLR, RPT	**Wrap HNDS at ankle**
	RPT all above	

SNAKE

LOF   Lying on stomach   HNDS on FLR at SHL

COUNTS	BODY MOVEMENT	ARMS
1-4	Push HNDS into FLR & arch BK	**Palms at SHLS**
5-8	RET to FLR	
1-24	RPT 3 Xs	
1-4	Lift legs with body on FLR	**Palms at pelvis**
5-8	RET legs to FLR	
1-24	RPT 3 Xs	THE SNAKE
1-32	Arch HNDS and legs off FLR	**Arms 2nd POS LJA**
	(Done 4 Xs)	

STRETCH FOR STRENGTHENING
SMALL OF BK AND UPPER THIGH MUSCLES

LOF   Stomach on FLR   HNDS holding onto ankles

COUNTS	BODY MOVEMENT
1-4	Pull legs up, arching BK (lift thighs off FLR)
5-8	Lower to FLR and hold 4 CTS
	RPT 3 Xs and hold in arched POS
	On stomach, rock FWD and back holding in arched POS. End by balancing on thighs — back straight — torso P.P. to FRT.

INVERTED BACK BEND

SIDE AND FORWARD SPLIT

SOF   Legs 2nd POS   (This exercise done only
after good warmup with legs in 2nd POS.)

COUNTS	BODY MOVEMENT
1-4 (Sl. Ct.)	**Lift pelvis off FLR, turn torso to R side and pulse while in split POS. R leg NTO, L leg TO. HNDS straddle R leg.**
5-8	**Lift torso to FWD split, HNDS front of body (FT flexed)**
1-4	**Lift torso to L side split**
5-8	**Lift torso to FWD split**
1-16	**RPT**
1-16	**Then lie FWD on stomach, leaving legs in 2nd POS. Hold in this POS for 8 CTS, then bring legs together slowly.**
	RPT
	Exercise must be done slowly.

SIDE SPLIT

PLIES DONE IN TURNED OUT POSITION, ALSO WITHOUT TURN OUT (parallel or neutral position)

CB   (Standing, FT in 1st — Plies, TO)

COUNTS	BODY MOVEMENT	ARMS
1-2	**Demi-plie**	**Arms 1st POS**
3-4	**Releve keeping knees flexed ("plie-releve" POS)**	**Move to 2nd LJA**
5-6	**In releve, STR**	**Same**
7-8	**Lower heels to FLR**	**Arms press to 1st**
1-2	**Releve**	**Same as above**
3-4	**"Plie-releve" POS**	
5-6	**Heels to FLR**	
7-8	**Lock knees**	

"PLIE-RELEVE" POSITION

RPT — 2nd POS plie	**Arms 2nd POS**
RPT — 4th POS plie	**L arm FWD, R arm 2nd**
RPT — 5th POS plie	**Arms FWD (SHL height). Palms pushing front, elbows locked.**
REV 4th and 5th POS	
These plies are also in P.P. (NTO)	**Arms flex at wrists.**
Use slow CTS of 8.	
(also grande plie at end of each POS)	

"Muscles should be elastic."

1PF   1ST POSITION FINGERS

Flat Hand, palms facing any direction

COUNTS	BODY MOVEMENT	ARMS
	Begin 4th POS demi-plie	1PF throughout, heel of HND to BK, HNDS to BK, HNDS on pelvis
1-2	Step side R demi-plie PP	Thrust R HND 2nd POS
3-4	Close L to R 1st PP	Thrust L HND 2nd POS
5-6	Step R FWD	R arm swings FWD (BK of HND to audience)
7-8	Close L to R 1st PP	L arm swings FWD (BK of HND to audience)
1-2	Step R BK	R arm swings down-palm FRT
3-4	Close L to R 1st PP	L arm swings down-palm FRT
5-6	XROL	LJA 2nd POS
7&8	3/4 OTL	Chest PDBras to ILJA
1-16	Repeat all above to L	Same as above to L side

2PF/JH   2ND POSITION FINGERS   JAZZ HAND

Fingers & thumb stretched to fullest open position, palms facing any direction

COUNTS	BODY MOVEMENT	ARMS
	Begin 4th POS demi-plie	HNDS on pelvis-1PF
1-2	Pique R FWD to 4th POS	X Arms FWD (&) Cut ELBs
3-4	Close L to R FA 1st PP	JH 2nd POS (2PF)
5-6	Pique R BK to 4th POS	Same as CTS 1-2
7-8	Close L to R to FA 1st PP	Same as CTS 3-4
1-2	Passe NEUT R XROL to 4th POS C#2-HD FRT	R JH on hip (2PF) L JH EXD TO C#2 from fist (3PF)
3-4	Passe NEUT L XLOR to 4th POS C#1-HD FRT	L JH on hip (2PF) R JH EXD to C#1
5-6	Plie to BK 2nd POS	JH 2nd POS
7-8	Turn R (Spiral) to 4th POS-R FRT	Fist at SHL (3PF) JH DIAG down (2PF)
1-16	Repeat all above to L	Same as above to L side

3PF 3RD POSITION FINGERS

Clenched fist, HND facing any direction

COUNTS	BODY MOVEMENT	ARMS
	Begin 4th POS demi-plie, R FRT	HNDS on pelvis (1PF)
1	Tap R to 1st PP	Fists into SHLS
2	XROL	L DIAG down, R ELB bent (3PF)
3-4	Tap L to 1st PP, XLOR	Fists into SHLS, R DIAG down, L ELB bent
5&6	Step BK R-L-R	Thrust R FWD from SHL (5), thrust L FWD (&)
7&8	Hold 4th POS (L FT FWD) AST CON	L fist at L SHL
	(CT 7), REL (&), CON (8)	R fist thrust FWD 2 X's
1-8	Repeat above to L	Same as above to L

4PF 4TH POSITION FINGERS WRIST FLEX

HND bends at wrist, fingers together, palms facing any direction. HND may bend up or down. Important: Do not hyperextend at elbow—hold from bicep and tricep.

COUNTS	BODY MOVEMENT	ARMS
	Begin 4th POS demi-plie, R FRT	HNDS on pelvis (1PF)
1-2	Lunge R Fwd to TI 4th POS (L Leg PP FA)	Both Wrist Press FWD (ELBS 2nd)
3-4	Close R to L 1st PP	Both Wrist Press down
5-6	¼ turn to L facing S#6 Lunge R FWD to TI 4th POS	Both Wrist Press FWD
7-8	Close R to L 1st PP	Both Wrist Press down
1-2	½ turn to L facing S#8 Lunge R FWD to TI 4th POS	Both Wrist Press FWD
3-4	Close R to L 1st PP	Both Wrist Press down
5-6	Step BK L demi-plie	L Wrist Press OVHD
7-8	Step BK R demi-plie	R Wrist Press OVHD
1-16	Repeat all above to L	Same as above to L

5PF   FIFTH POSITION FINGERS   FINGER FAN

Begin 3PF. Open thumb, then index, etc. to little finger. Return with little finger & end with thumb as a fan (then 3PF).

COUNTS	BODY MOVEMENT	ARMS
	Begin 4th POS demi-plie, R FRT	HNDS on pelvis (1PF)
1-2	Step R to 2nd POS	R Fist lift to 2nd
		L HND on pelvis
3-4	XLOR	Fan R (5PF)
5-6	Step R BKf	Close R HND to fist at SHL
&7	Step L -XROL	Fan both (R-L) 2nd POS
&8	Hold POS	Fan BK to fist at sides
1-8	Repeat all above to L	Same as above to L

6PF   6TH POSITION FINGERS   BUTTERFLY FINGERS

Thumb pressed to middle finger—little finger up. Other fingers extended, palms facing any direction.

COUNTS	BODY MOVEMENT	ARMS
	Begin 4th POS demi-plie, R FRT	6PF at sides
1-2	Pique R FWD to S#5	R arm OVHD thru SHL
3-4	XLOR demi-plie C#1	Press FWD DIAG C#1 (6PF)
		L above SHL (ELB bent) (6PF)
5-6	Same as CTS 1-2 to S#8	Same as above
7-8	Same as CTS 3-4 to C#4	Same as above
1-2	Same as CTS 1-2 to S#7	Same as above
3-4	Same as CTS 3-4 to C#3	Same as above
5&6	½ Turn R to face FRT—Step R-L-R to 4th POS demi-plie	Both arms to SHLS 6PF Palms FWD
7&8	Hold POS	Wrist circle down holding butterfly fingers
1-16	Repeat all above to L	Same as above to L

7PF   7TH POSITION FINGERS   BALLET FINGERS

All fingers have their own identity. There is strength but no tension—palms can face any direction.

COUNTS	BODY MOVEMENT	ARMS
	Begin 4th POS demi-plie, R FRT	**1PF at sides**
1-2	**Step R to 2nd POS**	**2nd POS -7PF**
3-4	**XLBR**	**ELB circle**
5-8	**Hold POS**	**Press arms to 5th en bas**
1-8	**Repeat all above to L**	**Same as above to L**

Grade *1*

Beginning Jazz Class

Floor Stretches

Note: *Lying on floor*

NECK VERTEBRAE STRETCH

LOF   Fingers interlaced at top
of skull   Elbows on FLR

COUNTS	BODY MOVEMENT	ARMS
1-4	**Pull HD FWD until elbows touch**	
5-8	**Relax and return HD to FLR**	
1-24	**RPT 3Xs**	

NECK VERTEBRAE STRETCH

CONTRACTION EXERCISE
(For Strengthening Middle Back)

LOF   Arms 2nd, Palms DWN
FT in parallel 2nd, knees flexed
Exercise done to build strength for the contraction series.

COUNTS	BODY MOVEMENT	ARMS
1-2	**Contract torso**	**R arm crosses TWD L knee**
3-6	**Hold**	**R arm across**
7-8	**Return to FLR**	**R arm 2nd on FLR**
1-8	**REV L**	
1-8	**RPT using both arms AST**	

This is also done with a develope leg.
Develope L leg with R arm, both legs with both arms.

BOTH LEGS EXTENDED—
SMALL OF BACK INTO FLOOR

TORSO TWIST

LOF   Arms 1st POS   Palms DWN
Legs STR   Toes PTD

COUNTS	BODY MOVEMENT
1-2	**Lift pelvis TWD ceiling** **(Heels and SHLS and palms on FLR)**
3-4	**Twist torso R**
5-6	**Return to center**
7-8	**Return to FLR**
1-8	**RPT L**
1-16	**RPT above**

Exercise also performed twisting R&L
before returning to FLR.

TORSO LIFT NEUTRAL POSITION

"Begin with basic relaxing exercises."

LOW CONTRACTIONS

LOF   Arms 2nd POS   Palms DWN
Legs STR   Toes PTD

COUNTS	BODY MOVEMENT	ARMS
1	CON torso & HD. Flex knees & FT.	Jazz HNDS 2nd POS
2-4	Hold	
5-6	Hold CON. Straighten knees & FT. (Small of back into FLR.)	LJA 2nd POS
7-8	Return to FLR	Return to FLR
1-24	RPT 3 Xs	

LOW CONTRACTION   STRAIGHT LEGS BACK INTO FLOOR

POINT AND FLEX DEVELOPPE

LOF   Arms 2nd POS Palms DWN
Legs STR   Toes PTD

COUNTS	BODY MOVEMENT	ARMS
1	Lift R leg slightly, toe PTD	2nd POS
2	R knee to tabletop	
3-4	Developpe R to ceiling	
5-6	Return to tabletop	
7	Extend leg FWD	
8	Return to FLR	
1-8	RPT L — point	
1-8	RPT with both legs AST — point	
1-8	RPT R with flexed FT — flex	
1-8	RPT L with flexed FT — flex	
1-8	RPT both with flexed FT — flex	
1-2	R to tabletop with toe PTD — PT	
3-4	Developpe to ceiling with flexed FT — flex	
5-6	Return to tabletop with toe PTD — PT	
7	Extend R FWD with flexed FT — flex	
8	Return R to FLR with toe PTD	
1-8	RPT on L	
1-8	RPT R and L AST	
1-24	RPT the above 24 CTS (Flex-Point)	

TABLE TOP LEG

"The best tranquilizer in the world is exercise."

WAIST TWIST

Stretch for BK of leg and stomach side
muscles with legs extended overhead
LOF   Arms 2nd POS   Palms DWN

COUNTS	BODY MOVEMENT	ARMS
1-4	Bring both knees into the chest — PT toes	
5,6,7	Extend legs to ceiling, locking knees	
8	Flex ankles	
1-4	Legs move to R side (from hips). Do not touch FLR with FT.	SHLS remain on FLR
5-8	Return legs to vertical POS	
1-4	Legs move to L side	
5-8	Return legs to vertical POS	
1-6	Lower legs to FLR. PT and flex FT.	
7-8	Open 2nd POS. Close 1st and touch FLR. RPT 3 Xs	

WAIST TWIST

BATTEMENT LEG STRETCH

LOF   Arms 2nd POS   Palms DWN

COUNTS	BODY MOVEMENT	ARMS
1-2	R leg battement 90°, PT toe, knee locked	Arms 2nd, palms on FLR
3-4	Flex knee and ankle. Grip toes.	
5-8	Bring knee to chest	Interlace fingers BK of leg
1-6	Straighten leg, PT Toe. (Keep close to chest.)	Same
7-8	Return leg to FLR	
1-16	Reverse	
	RPT exercise R&L	CONTROLLED FLEX OF KNEE AND ANKLE, GRIP TOES

LEGS UP, LEGS DWN

LOF   Arms 2nd POS

COUNTS	BODY MOVEMENT	ARMS
1-7	Lift legs to 90°, knees locked	2nd POS, palms DWN
8	Flex FT	
1-8	Lower legs to FLR, FT flexed (Small of BK must remain into FLR.)	
1-48	RPT 3 Xs	

BACK REMAINS INTO FLOOR
THROUGHOUT EXERCISE

FEET SOLE TO SOLE—Frog POS

SOF   Feet Sole to Sole

COUNTS	BODY MOVEMENT	ARMS
1-16	Round the back & pulse FWD	HNDS on ankles
1-2	Scoop—heels off FLR	V POS
3-4	Sit square and stretch legs FWD	Press 2nd LJA
1-16	Round BK and pulse FWD	Reach past FT
1-4	Scoop and press open legs 2nd	V POS to 2nd
1-16	Round BK and pulse FWD	2nd POS over ankles
1-4	Scoop and Press. Close legs, flex FT.	
1-16	Pulse FWD	
1-4	Scoop and Press, FT sole to sole	
1-48	RPT from top pulse 8 CTS	
1-32	RPT with 4 CTS of pulses	
1-24	RPT with 2 CTS for pulses	
1-12	RPT pulse, scoop, press in each POS	
1-36	RPT last 12 CTS 3 Xs	

FROG POSITION
WITH ROUNDED BACK

CONTRACT TO SQUARE

LOF   Arms 2nd POS   Palms DWN
Legs STR   Toes PTD

COUNTS	BODY MOVEMENT	ARMS
1-4	CON to square	1, 2 JH & LJA 3, 4
5-8	Pulse FWD over legs	Reach past FT, V POS
1-2	Scoop torso FWD over legs	V POS OVRHD
3-4	Sit square	Press 2nd LJA
5-8	CON to FLR	5, 6 JH & LJA 7, 8
1-48	RPT 3 Xs	

FORWARD PULSE, BACK STRAIGHT,
ARMS V POSITION OVERHEAD

STRETCH FOR FEET—For better body circulation

SOF   Legs 1st POS   BK STR
HNDS on FLR for support   Knees locked   Toes PTD

COUNTS	BODY MOVEMENT
1-2	Knees flex, flex ankles, grip toes.
3-4	Straighten knees and ankles, open toes.
5-8	Circle feet out and bring them together in flexed POS — PT CT 8
	RPT 8 Xs
1-2	Flex R ankle and knee
3-4	Flex L ankle and knee, R straighten
5-6	Flex R & L
7-8	Straighten and PT R & L
1-16	RPT

FLEX KNEES, ANKLES
AND TOES GRIPPED

STRAIGHTEN KNEES AND
OPEN TOES TO A POINT

STRENGTHENING BUTTOCKS

SOF   Keeping the knees locked

COUNTS	BODY MOVEMENT	ARMS
1-16	Walk FWD on the buttocks and then BKWD, toes are PTD, knees locked. Use hip socket for movement	Arms 2nd POS, LJA
	RPT	
	Exercise done slowly, then at faster speed	

PASSE DEVELOPPE—Turned Out

SOF   Arms 2nd POS—Feet 1st POS

COUNTS	BODY MOVEMENT	ARMS
1	Lift R leg 6″ off FLR (BK STR throughout)	2nd POS, palms DWN
2	Passe R TO	
3-4	Developpe R 2nd POS	
5-6	Fan R leg to 1st	
7-8	Battement R and DWN to FLR	
1-8	RPT L	
1-16	RPT R & L	
	This may also be done with a flexed foot on the developpe.	
1-8	Also done with both legs (frog POS on CT 2, heels off FLR).	

PASSE POSITION—TURNED OUT

2nd POS STRETCH

SOF   Feet parallel 2nd on FLR   Arms 2nd POS

COUNTS	BODY MOVEMENT	ARMS
1	Place R HND on instep of R FT over torso	R HND on R FT
2-4	Lock & stretch R leg to 2nd POS with toe PTD	
5-8	Relax R leg	
1-4	Lock & stretch R leg to 2nd with FT flexed	
5-8	Relax R leg	
1-16	RPT above	
1-32	RPT L	
1-32	RPT R & L AST	
1-4	Stretch both legs 2nd POS, toes PTD	
5-8	Pulse legs to FLR	
1-8	Flex FT, continue pulse to FLR	
1-4	Release HNDS, hold legs in POS	
5-8	Fan both legs to first POS	
1-4	Lift legs to ceiling — V POS, sit	OVRHD V POS
5-8	Return both legs to FLR	

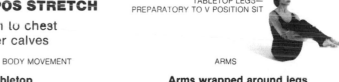

PREPARATION FOR 2ND
POSITION STRETCH

CALVES BOUNCE—Relaxation and Circulation
SOF   Legs in 1st POS   Palms on FLR next to buttocks

COUNTS	BODY MOVEMENT	ARMS
1-16	Bounce calves on FLR to relax leg	
1-16	Bounce to 2nd and return	Arms 2nd
	RPT all above	

TABLETOP—V POS STRETCH

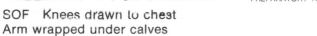

TABLETOP LEGS—
PREPARATORY TO V POSITION SIT

SOF   Knees drawn to chest
Arm wrapped under calves

COUNTS	BODY MOVEMENT	ARMS
1-4	Lift legs to tabletop	Arms wrapped around legs
5-8	Balance	
1-8	Return legs to FLR, RELX BK	At sides
1-8	Lift FT to V POS	Hands at ankles
	Round BK HD to knees	
1-16	Straighten BK square POS and sit knees together, FT 1st at buttocks	Arms 2nd POS, LJA
1-4	Legs to tabletop	Arms 2nd, LJA
5-8	Return legs to FLR round the BK	
1-8	Relax BK with HD on knees	Arms at sides
	RPT from beginning	

KNEEL AND RELAX WITH ROUNDED VERTEBRAE

Kneel and sit on your heels   HD on FLR

COUNTS	BODY MOVEMENT	ARMS
1-8	Hold in rounded POS	Arms on FLR, next to legs, HNDS by heels
1-4	Torso contracted, lift to sitting POS	HNDS on FLR
1-4	Push through pelvis and arch your BK	HNDS on FLR behind body
1-4	Release buttocks, sit on heels. Release rib-cage, return to starting POS with HD on FLR Exercise done 4 Xs	

FETAL POSITION

Barre Stretches

Note: Done at the barre

FORWARD BEND, GRANDE PLIE, ARCH BACK (Body Roll)

AB   Face barre   Hold on to barre with
both HNDS   FT 2nd NTO

COUNTS	BODY MOVEMENT
1-4	Bend FWD from hips
5	Grande-plie (FT and knees remain in 2nd PP)
6-8	Push pelvis through, arch BK and lift body to standing POS.

RPT all of above 4 Xs

RPT above again 4 Xs, done at a faster rhythm

Full exercise done in 4 CTS, 2 bend, plie and up.)

Balance at end of exercise. Arms OVRHD.

ARCH BACK AND LIFT BODY

FORWARD BEND, CONTRACT AND RELEASE RIB-CAGE, PELVIS AND HEAD

AB   Face Barre   Hold on to barre with both HNDS
FT 2nd POS NTO   Body is bent from hips and chest
is parallel to FLR

COUNTS	BODY MOVEMENT
1-4	CON (round BK for 4 CTS) rib-cage (Stop at neutral when changing from CON to REL)
5-8	Release (arch BK for 4 CTS) rib-cage

RPT above 4 Xs

RPT above again 4 Xs, at faster rhythm
(Contract 2 CTS, release 2 CTS.)

Also add pelvis and HD, contraction and release.

ARCH BACK—RELEASE
HEAD AND PELVIS

"A head atop a long neck, a slim body in leotard and tights, muscularly defined legs, feet flying from the floor . . . to those sitting in a darkened theatre watching a brightly lit stage, dancers are magic. With their bodies they can tell stories, create moods and express desires."

RELEVE, GRANDE PLIE,
PELVIS LIFT AND ARCH BACK (Body Roll)

AB   LFT HND on barre   Body turned so L side is facing
barre   FT 2nd NTO   R arm OVRHD   Jazz HND

COUNTS	BODY MOVEMENT	ARMS
1-2	Releve	
3-4	Grande-plie (vertebrae STR, buttocks) under rib-cage	
5,6,7	Push pelvis FWD, arch BK, body lift to releve POS	R arm circles BK and returns OVRHD
8	Place heels on FLR	
	(RPT 4 Xs. Last time hold in releve for 8 CTS. Take both HNDS off of barre and lift above HD and balance.)	
	(REV above to R side, R HND on barre, etc.)	

ARCH BACK AND BODY LIFT

FORWARD BEND, CONTRACT AND
RELEASE STOMACH MUSCLES

AB   Face and hold barre with both HNDS
FT 2nd POS NTO   Tabletop BK   Chest parallel to FLR

CON and release stomach muscles, 4 CTS for each.
Add rib-cage and CON and release.
Add SHLS and pelvis, CON and release.
Add HD, CON and release. (At end of exercise
diminish CTS, consequently contracting and
releasing to lesser CTS.)

TABLETOP BACK

GRANDE PLIE SECOND POSITION, SWING
TORSO OVER RIGHT LEG AND LEFT LEG

AB   Face and hold barre with both HNDS
FT 2nd POS TO

COUNTS	BODY MOVEMENT
1-4	Bounce in deep 2nd POS, swing torso
5-8	Over R FT, flex L FT, lock L knee. Bounce.
1-4	Return to 2nd POS
5-8	Bounce, Reverse to L side
1-4	And bounce. Return to center.
5-8	And bounce. Releve and balance at end with arms OVRHD. Use four slow CTS for each movement.

LUNGE OVER RIGHT FOOT, FLEX LEFT

BACK BEND WITH LEG EXTENDED BACK

AB   Face and hold barre with both HNDS
R FT BK 4th POS NTO   Knees locked
Lift R arm off barre OVRHD   Arch BK into BK bend
Close 1st POS and reverse to L FT BK

COUNTS   BODY MOVEMENT

1-16   Exercise may be done lifting both arms OVRHD
Exercise also done in plie-releve POS
Use four slow CTS for each movement

BACK BEND USING ARMS

STRETCH HAMSTRING AND PASSE

AB   Face and hold barre with both HNDS
R FT BK 4th POS NTO   Bounce R heel to FLR (stretch
muscles in back of leg)   Passe R leg, passe L leg
Place L FT 4th POS BK   Bounce L heel to FLR

8 CTS R, 8 CTS L
RPT — Use four CTS, then diminish to two CTS.

HAMSTRING (Back of Knee)
STRETCH

LEG SWINGS FORWARD AND BACK

AB   L HND on barre   R arm 2nd POS   FT 1st POS TO
R leg swings in attitude POS FWD and BK
Balance at end of leg swing   Remove HNDS from
barre
(Swings are done with supporting leg locked,
then plie-lock supporting leg, then plie-releve.)
Use 8 CTS for leg swing.

AB   Leg Swings — Across body and 2nd POS.
Same swing as above with different direction.
Locked knee, plie-lock, plie-releve.

Change to L leg swing

LEG SWING,
BACK ATTITUDE POSITION

PLIE, RELEASE AND CONTRACT, RIB-CAGE, PELVIS AND HEAD

AB   Left HND on barre   FT 2nd NTO
Legs remain in plie all during this exercise
R arm in 2nd POS   Chest parallel to FRT wall

COUNTS	BODY MOVEMENT	ARMS
1-4	Release pelvis and HD (sway BK, facing ceiling).	
5-8	Contract (push pelvis FWD, face looks at FLR, round vertebrae). Legs must remain in plie for release and contraction.	
	RPT above 4 Xs at faster rhythm, done in 4 CTS, 2 CTS release, 2 CTS contract.	

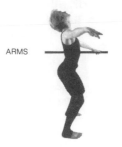

RELEASED PELVIS AND HEAD

ATTITUDE LEG SWINGS, HOLD LEG SECOND POSITION

AB   L HND on barre   Leg swings
FT 2nd TO   R arm in 2nd POS

COUNTS	BODY MOVEMENT	ARMS
1-2	R leg in attitude swings across body	
3-4	R leg swing to 2nd POS attitude	
5-8	RPT	
1-8	Hold R leg in 2nd POS, lift L arm OVRHD — palm front	R arm remains in 2nd, palm front — balance
1-4	Plie L leg, R leg remains in attitude in 2nd	
5-8	Releve L FT, L knee remains in plie	
1-4	Grande-plie, 2nd POS, arms 2nd, palms front	
5-8	Lock knees, FT remain in 2nd, arms move to first, at side of body.	
	RPT above 4 Xs.	
	REV above to L side, R HND on barre, etc.	

ATTITUDE LEG SWING
ACROSS BODY

PLIE, PASSE, LEG EXTENDS
FORWARD AND SECOND POSITION

AB   L HND on barre   PT R toe BK   Contract body
Start FT 1st POS NTO   R arm at R side

COUNTS	BODY MOVEMENT	ARMS
1	PT R toe BK, plie L leg (L leg remains in plie for entire exercise)	R arm to 2nd, LJA
2	Bring R FT to L knee (Passe POS), body contracts	R arm swings to jazz HND 2nd, from SHL
3-4	Develope R leg FWD, L leg plie	R arm remains 2nd, LJA
5-6	Swing R leg 2nd POS	
7	Lift R leg to its fullest 2nd extension	
8	Close R leg in 1st POS, knees locked	1st POS
1-24	RPT above 3 Xs	
	REV above to L side, R HND on barre, etc.	

FOOT AT PASSE POSITION

BACK BEND

AB   Facing barre   Both hands holding
on to barre   FT in 1st NTO

COUNTS	BODY MOVEMENT	ARMS
1-2	Releve	
3-6	Arch back, keep pelvis at barre and BK bend	
7-8	Return to standing POS with heels on FLR	
	RPT above 4 Xs	
	Exercise is done slowly.	

BACK BEND

FORWARD BEND FROM HIPS

AB   BK to barre   Bend from hips
Fingertips on FLR   FT in 2nd POS NTO

COUNTS	BODY MOVEMENT	ARMS
1-16	Relax and push palms of HNDS to FLR 16 Xs. Knees must remain locked.	HNDS on FLR
	RPT above with FT 1st POS NTO	
	Relax HD and neck muscles during exercise. Let blood circulate through skull.	

FORWARD BEND

PULSE SECOND POSITION, GRANDE PLIE, SIDE STRETCH AND BACK BEND

GRANDE PLIE— SECOND POSITION

AB   L HND on the barre   FT 2nd TO

COUNTS	BODY MOVEMENT	ARMS
1-4	Grande Plie	R arm in 2nd, LJA
1-8	Bounce in Grande-plie	Same
1-4	Come up slowly and lock knees	
1-4	FT TO releve	R arm lifts OVRHD, jazz HND
5-8	Bend FWD from buttocks with STR BK and HD (tabletop)	
1-4	Rise slowly to standing POS, lifting with STR BK	
5-8	Side stretch away from barre (in releve)	R 2nd, L over head off barre
1-4	Lift to standing POS	L HND on barre
5-8	BK bend releve	R second
1-4	Return to standing POS	
5-8	Lower heels	Lower arm to 1st POS
	Done 2 Xs on R side and 2 Xs on L side	

STRETCH FOR HAMSTRING, FRONT UPPER THIGH MUSCLES AND ACHILLES (Heel) TENDON

AB   Facing barre   FT 2nd NTO

COUNTS	BODY MOVEMENT	ARMS
1-4	Bounce into the barre, stretching ham string and achilles tendon. Keep hips FWD, heels DWN.	Both HNDS on barre during exercise.
5-8	Pull away from barre bouncing, lift buttocks	
1-8	RPT	
1-8	RPT again	STRETCH FOR HAMSTRING, THIGH AND ACHILLES
1-4	Pull away from barre with buttocks, into sitting POS with STR BK heels, releve.	
1-2	Lock pelvis, place knees on FLR (stretch thighs)	
3-4	Return to sitting POS	
5-6	Lock pelvis, knees on FLR	
7-8	Return to sitting POS	
1-4	Body roll to standing POS pushing through with pelvis and arching BK	
5-8	Balance in releve	Arms OVRHD
1-4	Push heels into FLR	Lower arms to barre
	RPT all above	
	Exercise done 4 Xs	

SECOND POS BATTEMENT STRETCH, WITH LEG ON BARRE

AB   Facing barre   R leg on barre/hips parallel to wall, TO
Arms OVRHD   FT flexed

COUNTS	BODY MOVEMENT	ARMS
1-8	Turn and bend to R leg with STR BK	Arms OVRHD — V POS
1-8	Hold ankles, pulse	
1-4	Scoop and lift with STR BK to standing POS	Over head
5-8	Make ½ pivot on L, leg on barre in 2nd	Same
1-8	Side stretch over leg, PT toes	Same
1-4	Lift to standing POS	Arms in 2nd POS
5-8	Face barre	Arms in 1st POS
	RPT 2 Xs with R leg, 2 Xs with L leg	

LEG DIAGONAL LINE ON BARRE

FORWARD BEND FROM HIPS, FLEX AND LOCK KNEES WITH TABLETOP BACK

AB   L HND on the barre   FT in 2nd NTO
R arm OVRHD   Jazz HND

COUNTS	BODY MOVEMENT	ARMS
1-4	Bend FWD from hips with STR BK	R OVRHD
5-8	Plie knees FWD, chest parallel to FLR, lock knees on CT 8 (tabletop POS)	R arm swings down and BK
1-4	Plie knees FWD, chest parallel to FLR, lock knees on CT 4	Arm swings DWN & reaches front
5-8	Lock knees and return to standing POS	R arm returns to OVRHD
	RPT (exercise also done in releve)	
	Exercise done 4 Xs	

FORWARD BEND—TABLETOP BACK

"A moving body is renewing and rebuilding itself."

RELEVE AND GRANDE-PLIES

CB   1st POS TO
Standing POS   Arms at side

COUNTS	BODY MOVEMENT	ARMS
1-4	Releve	Arms lift to 2nd POS
5-8	Grande-plie (FT remain in releve, knees open to 2nd POS)	X FRT of chest and high 1st POS — lift to 2nd
1-4	Lock knees (lift torso to standing POS)	
5-8	Lower heels	Press to 1st
	Above exercise also done NTO (FT 6" apart)	
	RPT all in 2nd POS	
	Exercise done 4 Xs slowly	
	Also done 4th and 5th POS	

GRANDE PLIE—FIRST POSITION

DEMI-PLIE IN 4th POS WITH DIAGONAL ARM STRETCH

CB   4th POS TO   R FT FWD
Standing POS   Arms at sides

COUNTS	BODY MOVEMENT	ARMS
1-2	Demi-plie	Both HNDS into chest, elbow bent
3-4	Lock the knees	Arms move to over head, BK of HNDS FRT
5-6	Plie	Arms to DIAG POS—L FWD
7-8	Lock knees, R SHL to C#1	Arms press to 1st
	Done 4 Xs, reverse to L FT FWD	
	Also done lifting to releve and into plie-releve POS as arms move on diag.	
	Also done with parallel pull down	

DIAGONAL ARM STRETCH—
"PLIE-RELEVE" POSITION

SHOULDER LIFTS ARM MOVEMENT

CB   L leg FWD TO   Locked knee
R FT BK on half toe   Arms 1st POS

COUNTS	BODY MOVEMENT	ARMS
1-4	R shoulder lifts R arm with locked elbow to OVRHD POS	
5-8	R SHL pushes DWN, returns arm to side of body (wrist leads, HND trails)	
1-4	Step R 2nd POS, ISOL R knee TI R arm pushes FWD from 2nd POS, elbow locked, wrist leads, L arm at side	
5-8	R arm moves BK to 2nd POS, lock knee. Lead with elbow, palm DWN.	
	Reverse exercise to L side. Also diminish to lesser CTS	
	Exercise done 4 Xs each side	
	Also done with releve and Grande-plie	

SHOULDER
LIFTS
ARM

FORWARD BEND, RELAX AND PULSE

CB   Bend from hips, torso rounded

Knees locked   Feet POS parallel

RELAX PULSE

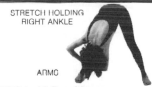

COUNTS	BODY MOVEMENT	ARMS
1-8	Bounce HNDS to FLR, let HD hang, exhale	
1-8		Stretch arms to ceiling (wrists and elbows TO), inhale
	Done with FT in 2nd POS, NTO (FT 6" apart)	
	Exercise done 4 Xs slowly	

TURNTABLE STRETCH

STRETCH HOLDING
RIGHT ANKLE

CB   (Turntable) FT in 2nd TO
Arms at side   Standing POS

COUNTS	BODY MOVEMENT	ARMS
1 (Slow)	Bounce head to R knee	HNDS hold R ankle
2	Bounce head to L knee	HNDS hold L ankle
3-6	Body makes complete circle L from waist (L side, BK, R side, front)	Arms OVRHD and move to 2nd
7-8	Contract and torso erect, standing POS	
	Reverse to L side	
	Exercise done 4 Xs each side	

JAZZ HAND AND SIDE STRETCH

CB   FT 2nd TO   Standing POS

COUNTS	BODY MOVEMENT	ARMS
1	Arms swing 2nd POS — clench fists	
2	Hold	Explode jazz HNDS 2nd
3-4	Side stretch R	Arms reach OVRHD — V POS and palms PP
5-6	Return to upright POS	Arms 2nd POS
7	Hold	LJA 2nd, palms up
8		Arms press to sides
	Reverse to L side	
	Exercise done 4 Xs each side	

SIDE STRETCH

PASSE, POINT AND FLEX EXTENSION

CB   1st POS NTO   Standing POS
Locked knees   Arms at sides

COUNTS	BODY MOVEMENT	ARMS
1-2	Lift R FT to passe at L knee NTO, PTD toe	Arms 2nd POS, Jazz HND
3-4	Extend R leg FWD, PTD toe	
5-6	Return R leg to passe at knee, NTO	
7-8	Step R FT on FLR, plie 8 NTO	Arms 1st POS
1-8	Reverse exercise to L leg	
1-2	Lift R FT to passe at L knee TO, PTD toe	Arms 2nd POS, jazz HND
3-4	Extend R leg to 2nd POS, PTD toe	
5-6	Return R leg to passe at knee, TO	
7-8	Passe FRT NTO, to FLR and plie	Arms 1st POS
	RPT exercise, extending leg BK to arabesque POS, from TO passe	
	Exercise may also be done flexing FT on CTS 3-4	
	Reverse all above L	

PASSE NEUTRAL POSITION

FEET SECOND POS, RELEASE AND CONTRACT RIB-CAGE, PELVIS AND HEAD

CB   FT 2nd POS NTO   Standing POS
Face side #8   Arms at sides

COUNTS	BODY MOVEMENT	ARMS
1-4	Release rib-cage, pelvis, HD and drop to FLR (exhale). Do not roll over on ankles.	**Arms at sides**
5-8	Contract rib-cage, pelvis, HD and return to standing POS (inhale)	**Arms at sides**
	Done 4 Xs	
	RPT and diminish to lesser CTS	
	(IMPORTANT: Heels remain on FLR during exercise.)	

RELEASE HEAD AND PELVIS

Jazz Isolations

Note: Done center floor

NECK ISOLATIONS

FT 2nd POS NTO   Standing POS
Stretch neck muscles BK and FWD

COUNTS	BODY MOVEMENT	ARMS
1-4	Looking down, stretching the muscles in the BK of the neck	Arms 1st POS
5-8	Look up, stretching muscles in FRT of the neck	

FT 2nd POS NTO   Standing POS
Stretch side neck muscles

RELEASE HEAD

1-4	Look sharply to the R side, keep HD high turning only the neck	Arms 1st POS
5-8	Look STR FWD	
	Reverse to L side (diminish to lesser CTS)	
1-8	Circle HD to the R, stretching as far as possible in each position. (Spot FLR, R side, ceiling, L side.) Keep eyes open. Reverse and circle L.	
1-8	Spot FWD, tilt HD R & L	
	Exercises are done slowly, then diminish to lesser CTS	
1-4	Spot FWD, swing HD R & L. Circle R and accent R on CT 4.	
5-8	REV — swing L, R and circle L	

SIDE STRETCH
OR TILT

SUNDARI HEAD MOVEMENTS (Oriental)
Head Isolation Forward

FT 2nd POS NTO   Standing POS

COUNTS	BODY MOVEMENT	ARMS
1-2	Thrust the HD FWD. Do not tilt the chin up or DWN. Face is parallel to front wall.	HNDS on pelvis
3-4	Return to neutral POS. (Diminish to lesser CTS.)	
5-8	RPT	
	RPT above 4 Xs	

FORWARD THRUST

SUNDARI HEAD MOVEMENTS
Head Isolation Back
FT 2nd POS NTO   Standing POS

COUNTS	BODY MOVEMENT	ARMS
1-2	Thrust HD BK. Do not tilt chin up or DWN. Face parallel to front wall.	HNDS on pelvis
3-4	Return to neutral POS. (Diminish to lesser CTS.)	
5-8	RPT	
	RPT above 4 Xs	

BACK THRUST

SUNDARI HEAD MOVEMENTS
Head Isolation R and L sides
FT 4th POS, R FT FWD on PT, plie supporting leg
Arms 2nd POS, lock elbows, push HNDS to walls

COUNTS	BODY MOVEMENT
1-2	Push HD to the R side. Do not lift or tilt HD.
3-4	Return to neutral POS
	Reverse to L side. (Diminish to lesser CTS.)
	Also move HD R & L without stopping at neutral
5-8	RPT
	RPT above 4 Xs

HEAD LEFT

SUNDARI HEAD MOVEMENTS
Head Isolation Square
FT 4th POS   R FT FWD on PT, plie supporting leg
Arms 2nd POS, lock elbows, push HNDS to walls

COUNTS	BODY MOVEMENT
1	Push HD FWD
2	Return to neutral POS
3-8	RPT pushing HD to the R, BK, and L
	Reverse to L side
1-8	REV all above L

"Curvature of the spine makes you look like you have a big bottom."

SUNDARI HEAD MOVEMENTS
Head Circle Isolation
FT 4th POS   R FT FWD on PT, plie supporting leg
Arms 2nd POS, lock elbows, push HNDS to walls

COUNTS	BODY MOVEMENT
1-4	Circle HD to the R, hitting all of the positions in between. Accent CT 4 by pushing the HD distinctly FWD.
5-8	Reverse circling L
1-24	Yes and NO — HD jiggle side to side
	RPT all above

FINGER ISOLATIONS
FT 4th POS NTO   Standing POS
Arms 1st POS   Stretch for jazz HND

COUNTS	BODY MOVEMENT
1-4	Arms move to 2nd POS, elbows flexed, clenched fist facing up, open fist fan fingers out, thumb to little finger. End with palm FWD.
5-8	Fan in, little finger to thumb. Return fists to chest. (Diminish to lesser CTS)
1-16	Fists at SHL — pull DWN to pelvis — open and stretch fingers — clench & return to SHL.

JAZZ HAND

SHOULDER ISOLATIONS
(Basic movements of the shoulder)
4th POS

COUNTS	BODY MOVEMENT	ARMS
1-2	Lift up—return to neutral	
3-4	Push FWD—neutral	
5-6	Pull DWN—return	
7-8	Pull BK—return	
1-4	½ circle FWD—return	
5-8	½ circle BK—return	
1-4	Full circle FWD	
5-8	Full circle BK	

SHOULDER LIFT

For shoulder isolations, FT 2nd POS, TO.   **Arms in 2nd POS, Jazz HNDS**
Practice each of above isolations,
alternating R arm, then L, then both arms.
SHL hits FWD & BK—R, L & both

SHOULDER ISOLATIONS

COUNTS	BODY MOVEMENT	ARMS
1	FT 2nd POS, TO standing POS. Knees locked.	Swing R arm 2nd POS, L HND on pelvis. Jazz HND, L arm remains 1st POS.
2		Isolate R shoulder, lifting up
3		Return R to CTR POS
4		ISOL R SHL, lifting up
5		Return SHL
6-7		Lift to LJA
8		Press to 1st POS

Reverse all to L side

Exercise also done using both arms and SHL ISOL

RPT using all SHL movements (FWD, BK & DWN)

Exercise is also done with jazz walks— 8 steps FWD and 8 BK — start R

JAZZ HAND
SECOND AND
ISOLATION RIGHT
SHOULDER UP

RIB-CAGE ISOLATIONS
Isolation R & L sides
FT 2nd POS TO   Standing POS
HNDS on FRT of pelvis

COUNTS	BODY MOVEMENT
1-2	Lift the rib-cage, place to R side
3-4	Return to CTR POS
5-8	RPT L side

RPT moving from R side to L side without stopping at CTR POS

Exercise also RPTS starting L side

Diminish to lesser CTS

RIB CAGE LEFT

RIB-CAGE ISOLATIONS
Release and Contract Rib-Cage
FT 2nd POS TO   Standing POS
HNDS on FRT of pelvis

COUNTS	BODY MOVEMENT

1-2 **Release rib-cage FWD (lift rib-cage to S#5)**

3-4 **Return to normal POS**

5-6 **Contract rib-cage BK (vertebrae is rounded pulling BK to S#7)**

7-8 **Return to normal POS**

RPT

Diminish to lesser CTS

RIB CAGE
CONTRACTION

RIB-CAGE ISOLATIONS
Rib-Cage Circle
FT 2nd POS TO   Standing POS
Arms OVRHD, V POS   Palms parallel

COUNTS	BODY MOVEMENT

1-2 **Release rib-cage FWD (lift rib-cage to S#5)**

3-4 **Lift rib-cage to R side**

5-6 **Contract rib-cage BK (vertebrae is rounded pulling BK to S#7)**

7-8 **Lift rib-cage to L side**

Reverse to L side

Diminish to lesser CTS

RIB CAGE
RIGHT SIDE

PELVIS ISOLATIONS
Contract and Release Pelvis
FT 2nd POS NTO   Standing POS
Demi-plie   Pelvis ISOL FWD and BK

COUNTS	BODY MOVEMENT	ARMS

1-2 **Contract—lift pelvis FWD**   **Arms in 2nd, jazz HND**

3-4 **Return to CTR POS**   **or on pelvis**

5-6 **Release—pull buttocks BK (S#7)**

7-8 **Return to CTR POS**

RPT. Diminish to lesser CTS.

RELEASE
PELVIS

PELVIS ISOLATIONS
Pelvis Hip Lift
FT 2nd POS NTO   Standing POS   Demi-plie

COUNTS	BODY MOVEMENT	ARMS
1-2	Lift hip to R side. (Do not lift heel or lock knees.)	Arms 2nd POS, jazz HND
3-4	Return to CTR POS	
5-6	Lift hip to R side again	
7-8	Return to CTR POS	
	Reverse all to L hip	
	RPT. Diminish to lesser CTS.	PELVIS SIDE RIGHT

PELVIS ISOLATIONS
Pelvis Square
FT 2nd POS NTO   Standing POS   Demi-plie

COUNTS	BODY MOVEMENT	ARMS
1-2	Contract pelvis FWD, return to neutral POS	Arms 2nd, jazz HND
3-4	Lift to R side, return to POS	
5-6	Release buttocks BK, return to POS	
7-8	Lift to L side, return to POS	
	Exercise also done as a circle without returning pelvis to neutral POS	
	Reverse. Diminish to lesser CTS.	
	Pelvis Hits — R side, Diag R, BK, Diag L, L side and return	
	Diminish also	

KNEE ISOLATIONS (Knee only)
Basic Movements of the Knee
(IMPORTANT: Do not roll over on side of working FT.)

COUNTS	BODY MOVEMENT	arms
1-2	Flex knee FWD, NTO, return to neutral	2nd POS, jazz HND
3-4	Flex knee out, TO	
5-6	Flex knee in, TI, return	
7	½ knee circle out	
8	½ knee circle in	
1-8	REV — RPT L knee	FLEX KNEE FRONT—NEUTRAL POSITION—HEEL LIFTED
	Also done lifting heel off FLR (See next exercise.)	

KNEE ISOLATION (Using knee and heel)

Lift heel of working leg, pressing ball of FT
into FLR. Other knee must remain locked.

COUNTS	BODY MOVEMENT	ARMS
1-2	**Flex R knee FWD, lifting heel**	**Arms 2nd POS, jazz HND**
3-4	**Return**	
5-6	**Flex R knee to TI POS, lifting heel**	
7-8	**Return**	
1-2	**Flex R knee to TO POS (to C#1) lifting heel**	
3-4	**Return**	
5-6	**½ knee circle to R side, lifting heel**	
7-8	**½ knee circle to L side, lifting heel**	
	Reverse. Diminish to lesser CTS.	

KNEE ROLL

FT 2nd POS TO   Standing POS   Knees locked
Arms 2nd POS   Palms parallel to FLR
(Lift heels off FLR. Do not roll over on sides of FT.)

COUNTS	BODY MOVEMENT
1-2	**Both knees make ½ circle to R, demi-plie**
3-4	**Both knees make ½ circle to L, demi-plie**
	RPT
	Above exercise also done using grande-plie.
	Exercise also done using a figure 8 pattern.

KNEE ROLL
STARTING TO RIGHT

Jazz Port de Bras

Note: Done center floor

JAZZ PORT DE BRAS COMBINATIONS

All of the following exercises may be done
with one arm at a time or any combination thereof
(except parallel arms, use both).

Stand with FT in 1st POS, NTO
Also may be done with walks:
Step R, L, R, L, FWD — 2 CTS for each step, RPT walking BK
Also done walking on each beat.

LONG JAZZ ARM

COUNTS	ARM MOVEMENT	HEAD MOVEMENT
1-4	Slowly lift arms to long jazz arm POS (2nd)	STR FWD, neutral POS
5-8	Slowly press arms DWN to sides	

LONG JAZZ ARM

INVERTED LONG JAZZ ARM

COUNTS	ARM MOVEMENT	HEAD MOVEMENT
1-4	Slowly lift arms to Inverted LJA POS (2nd—palms up)	STR FWD, neutral POS
5-8	Slowly press arms DWN to sides	

INVERTED LONG JAZZ ARM

V-POSITION ARM

COUNTS	ARM MOVEMENT	HEAD MOVEMENT
1-4	Slowly lift arms to OVRHD V-POS Palms parallel, fingers together	STR FWD, neutral POS
5-8	Slowly press arms DWN to sides	

There are 3 basic V positions:

1. **V POS DWN (FWD of pelvis)**
2. **V POS FRT (FWD of SHLS)**
3. **V POS OVRHD**

V POSITION OVERHEAD

CHEST

COUNTS	ARM MOVEMENT	HEAD MOVEMENT
1-2	Lift arms to 2nd POS LJA	STR FWD, neutral POS
3-4	Bring jazz HNDS into chest leaving elbows to 2nd, BK of HND to FRT	
5-6	Open to 2nd POS again	
7-8	LJA and DWN to sides	CHEST POSITION
1-8	RPT	
	May be done with percussive beat by moving arms on the beat	

CHEST AND PARALLEL ARM AND OPEN FWD

COUNTS	ARM MOVEMENT	HEAD MOVEMENT
1-2	Lift to 2nd LJA	STR FWD, neutral POS
3-4	Bring jazz HNDS into chest	
5-6	Raise to parallel POS OVRHD, back of HNDS FWD	BACK OF HAND PARALLEL
7-8	Pull parallel elbows DWN, thrust bK of HNDS FWD in PP	

DIAGONAL ARM STRETCH

COUNTS	ARM MOVEMENT	HEAD MOVEMENT
1-2	Lift to 2nd LJA	STR FWD
3-4	Bring jazz HNDS into chest, elbows 2nd	
5-6	PP OVRHD	Release HD slightly
7-8	R arm reaches FWD, L reaches BK (Step L, R on 7, 8 to REV to L side)	HD looks over L fingertips
		DIAGONAL ARMS

ARM SWING COMBINATION

COUNTS	ARM MOVEMENT	HEAD MOVEMENT
1-2	Lift arms to 2nd LJA	STR FWD
3-4	Swing arms across body low in FRT	
5-6	Swing open to 2nd	
7-8	Press DWN to 1st POS	
1-8	RPT	ARM SWING
	Above may be done individually with R and then L	

ARM SWING—OVERHEAD VARIATION

COUNTS	ARM MOVEMENT	HEAD MOVEMENT
1-2	Lift to 2nd LJA	STR FWD
3-4	Swing low across body in FRT	
5-6	Swing thru 2nd to OVRHD V-POS	
7-8	Press DWN to 1st POS thru 2nd POS	
1-8	RPT	OVERHEAD
	Above can be done individually with R and then L, also both	HALF V POSITION

ARM SWING AND THRUST TO 2nd POSITION

COUNTS	ARM MOVEMENT	HEAD MOVEMENT
1-2	Lift to 2nd LJA	STR FWD
3-4	Cross arms low in FRT of body	
5-6	Swing thru 2nd to OVRHD V-POS	
7 &	Circle HNDS into SHLS, elbows dropped. Then push palms and extend arms to 2nd.	
8	Press arms DWN to sides	HAND HEEL
1-8	RPT above	PRESS SECOND

CHEST AND ARM THRUST TO 2nd POSITION

COUNTS	ARM MOVEMENT	HEAD MOVEMENT
1-2	HNDS in to chest, elbows to 2nd	STR FWD
3-4	Open R to 2nd LJA	HD looks to FWD or R
5-6	Bring R into chest again	STR FWD
7	Thrust both to 2nd	Release slightly
8	Press both DWN to sides	
1-8	RPT	LONG JAZZ ARM
	(Step L, R on 7, 8 to REV to L side)	2ND POSITION AND CHEST

"Good posture counts in all movement."

ELBOW SWING AND BACK OF HAND THRUST

ELBOW SWING BACK

LEAD WITH
BACK OF HAND

COUNTS	ARM MOVEMENT
1-2	Swing R arm BK leading with elbow
3-4	Swing R to 2nd with BK of HND to FRT and 1st POS
5-8	REV above 4 CTS
1-8	Do exercise with both arms simultaneously

WRIST FAN

COUNTS	ARM MOVEMENT	HEAD MOVEMENT
1-2	Circle R fist away from body	STR FWD
3-4	Open R HND (like fan, start with R thumb) to jazz HND FRT	
5-8	RPT above 4 CTS	
1-8	RPT above 8 CTS	
	REV to L	

WRIST FAN

BACK DIAGONAL SHOULDER LEAD

COUNTS	ARM MOVEMENT	HEAD MOVEMENT
1-2	HNDS into chest, elbows 2nd	STR FWD
3-4	Drop elbows to PP and extend OVRHD	
5-6	Pull DWN to PP and to 1st POS	
7-8	Swing L BK on DIAG to C#4 (Lead with R SHL FWD)	Look over R SHL
1-8	RPT	
	Step L, R on 7, 8 to REV to other side	
	REV to L	

SHOULDER LEAD

ROCK WRIST CIRCLE

COUNTS	ARM MOVEMENT
& 1	Circle R wrist into SHL and push heel of HND to DIAG POS
& 2	Reverse
& 3	Circle R in and push on DIAG to C#1. ISOL R SHL FWD
& 4	Reverse
5-8	RPT above in 2nd
1-8	RPT above 8 CTS
	This exercise may be done to OVRHD POS and to the FLR
	REV to L

PRESS TO 2ND POSITION

ROCK ELBOW PULL BACK

COUNTS	ARM MOVEMENT	HEAD MOVEMENT
& 1	Pull R elbow BK with clenched fist	Release slightly
& 2	Pull L elbow BK	
& 3 & 4	Pull both BK on the beat	
5-8	RPT as above but in 2nd POS	
1-8	RPT all of above	

ELBOW PULL BACK

ROCK CROSS WRIST

COUNTS	ARM MOVEMENT
& 1	Cross arms FRT of chest — fists
& 2	Swing thru 2nd and cross wrists OVRHD
& 3	Swing thru 2nd and cross wrists FRT of chest again
& 4	Swing to 2nd and pull elbows BK
5-8	RPT above
1-8	RPT above 8 CTS

CROSS FRONT OF CHEST

WRIST CROSS AND
4th POSITION FUNKY

COUNTS   ARM MOVEMENT

& 1	Cross wrists FRT of body—fists clenched
& 2	Swing L OVRHD, R to 2nd
& 3 & 4	Reverse above 2 CTS
5-8	RPT
1-8	RPT above 8 CTS (add identical SHL to 2nd POS arm)

HIGH 4TH POSITION

ROCK PARALLEL SWING

COUNTS   ARM MOVEMENT

1	Swing both OVRHD—parallel
& 2	Swing FWD and DWN to parallel 1st
3 & 4	Swing R to BK DIAG, L SHL lead FWD, DWN CT 4
5-6	Swing both OVRHD and DWN as above
7 & 8	Swing L to BK DIAG, R SHL lead FWD
1-8	RPT as above

SWING RIGHT TO
BACK DIAGONAL

SHOULDER ROLL

COUNTS   ARM MOVEMENT

1	Roll R SHL BK, arms at sides — clenched fist of working arm
2	Roll L SHL BK
3-4	Pull R elbow BK to middle of BK, then L
5-8	RPT above 4 CTS
1-8	RPT above 8 CTS

SHOULDER LIFT

FUNKY TAP & CLAP

COUNTS	ARM MOVEMENT	HEAD MOVEMENT
& 1	**Tap R FT 2nd, circle R from SHL and to 2nd — L on pelvis**	**Pulses BK**
& 2	**Tap R FT next to L, clap HNDS at chest**	
& 3	**Tap R FT 2nd, circle R from SHL and to 2nd**	
4	**Close and step R to L, circle R at R hip and push DWN**	
& 5-8	**REV and RPt to L side**	
	May also be done using both arms AST	
	Also with wrist circle OVRHD or DWN to FLR	

FUNKY TAP

JAZZ WALK COMBINATIONS

Walks done in series of 8 CT progressions FWD and BKWD.
Start 2 CTS for each step, then diminish to 1 CT.

Each walk should be done 4 Xs so the students can correct themselves.

BOUNCE WALK

COUNTS	BODY MOVEMENT		ARM MOVEMENT
1	Step FWD R		Arms swing naturally—start L FWD, clenched fists or jazz HNDS
2	Plie on R with L in neutral passe		
3-4	RPT to L		
	(8 CTS FWD and 8 CTS BK)		Arms 1st POS on WLK BK

BOUNCE WALK

TAP STEP

COUNTS	BODY MOVEMENT	ARM MOVEMENT
1	Tap R toe FWD	LJA 2nd POS
2	Step R FWD plie	Arms cross FRT of chest
3-4	RPT to L	
	Do 8 CTS FWD and 8 CTS BK	
	(Also done in releve and with HD thrust FWD on CT 1 and back to neutral on CT 2.)	
	Also yes, no and side jiggle.	

LONG JAZZ ARM 2ND POSITION

TAP STEP WITH CONTRACTION AND RELEASE OF RIB-CAGE

COUNTS	BODY MOVEMENT	ARM MOVEMENT
1-2	FT same as above. Rib-cage contracts on CT 1 and releases on CT 2	CT 1 arms open to 2nd POS, jazz HNDS. LJA 2nd POS, CT 2.
3-8	Reverse and RPT	
1-8	Walk BK (R, L, R, L)	

TAP AND CONTRACT

JAZZ WALK—FRONT WITH CATCH STEP

COUNTS	BODY MOVEMENT	ARM MOVEMENT
1 & 2	CT 1, step R FT FRT (same as previous). Take a catch step on CTS & 2. (Catch step is two quick steps—in this case a quick LR moving FWD. Also called ball-change in tap.)	LJA CT 1, jazz HNDS 2nd POS on CT 2
	REV combination by starting on L FT.	
	Also done adding SHL ISOL on CTS 2, 4, 6, 8	L, R, L, R SHL

"PLIE-RELEVE" POSITION

PASSE STEP BACK

(To be used for a BKWD walk)

COUNTS	BODY MOVEMENT	ARM MOVEMENT
1	Passe R (releve) TO	Arms 2nd POS, LJA
& 2	Extend R leg to BK and step BK (plie)	
3 & 4	Reverse to L	
5-8	RPT	
	REV to L	

ARABESQUE

JAZZ WALK (Flat Foot)

COUNTS	BODY MOVEMENT	ARM MOVEMENT
1-8	FT in 1st POS, NTO, demi-plie. Place R FT (step on whole FT, ball and heel) FRT of L FT. Continue walk in STR line by placing L FT in FRT of R FT. Emphasis placed on keeping knees in demi-plie POS, BK STR, HD up continuing a STR line walk. (2 CTS for each step)	Arm reaches FWD in opposite to foot

JAZZ WALK FLAT

WRIST ISOLATION WALKS

COUNTS	BODY MOVEMENT	ARM MOVEMENT
1-2	Step R FWD	L wrist moves FWD in low POS, fingers trail
3-4	RPT to L	Wrist moves BK
5-8	RPT R and L Done 8 CTS FWD and 8 CTS BK	
1-16	RPT with L wrist	
1-16	RPT walks FWD and BK	Wrist leads arm up to SHL height and DWN
1-16	RPT walks FWD and BK	Wrist leads to OVRHD and DWN
1-16	RPT walks	L wrist moves across body in low POS and leads out again with BK of wrist
1-16	RPT walks	RPT with L
1-16	RPT walks	Both wrists across body (fingers trail)
1-16	RPT walks	RPT sequence with wrists at small of BK
1-16	RPT walks	R wrist circles OVRHD (circles in, out)
1-16	RPT walks	L wrist circles OVRHD (circles in, out)
1-16	RPT walks	Both wrists circle OVRHD (circles in, out)

WRIST
FORWARD

WRIST
BACK

SPIDER WALK

COUNTS	BODY MOVEMENT	ARM MOVEMENT
1-8	2 CT walk (R, L, R, L) (As R steps FWD, L is in BK attitude, TO, reverse)	2nd POS, jazz HND, roll HNDS & SHLS FWD on CTS 1, 3, 5 & 7

BACK ATTITUDE AND
SHOULDER ISOLATION

JAZZ WALK (Releve Foot)

COUNTS	BODY MOVEMENT	ARM MOVEMENT
1-8	FT in 1st POS, NTO, demi-plie. Place R FT (step on whole FT, ball & heel) in FRT of releve L FT. Place L flat in FRT of releve FT. Continue walking in STR line. (2 CTS for each step)	Arm reaches FWD in opposition to FT

JAZZ WALK—
RELEVE BACK FOOT

FUNKY WALK

COUNTS	BODY MOVEMENT	ARM MOVEMENT
& 1	Step R FWD (REL pelvis)	Cross arms FRT of chest
2	Tap L 2nd plie R (REL pelvis)	HNDS swing out next to SHLS
3-8	REV and RPT	

FUNKY WALK—
RELEASE PELVIS

LOW JAZZ WALK

COUNTS	BODY MOVEMENT	ARM MOVEMENT
1-8	FT in 1st POS, NTO, demi-plie. Body on 90° angle with chest parallel to FLR. HD up, face looking FRT. Step FWD on R FT, placing it FRT of L FT. Step FWD L FT, placing FRT of R. Continue walking FWD. (Walks may also be done releve BK FT as other FT steps FWD.) (2 CTS for each step)	Arm reaches FWD in opposition to FT, jazz HNDS

LOW JAZZ WALK

POPCORN WALK

COUNTS	BODY MOVEMENT	ARM MOVEMENT
1-8	Walk FWD R, L, R, L flat FT. Knees remain in plie and bounce on every CT (1-8). 2 CTS for each step.	Arms opposition—start L arm FWD, R arm 2nd
1-8	Same bounce walk BK	

POPCORN WALK

HIGH JAZZ WALK

COUNTS	BODY MOVEMENT	ARM MOVEMENT
1-8	FT in 1st POS, NTO, knees locked. With releved R FT step across releved L FT (cross to R DIAG); step releved L FT across releved R FT. Continue walking FWD. (2 CTS for each step)	Arm reaches FWD in opposition to FT, jazz HNDS

RELEVE WALK

SIDE JAZZ WALK

COUNTS	BODY MOVEMENT	ARM MOVEMENT
1-8	FT 1st POS, NTO, demi-plie. Step R FT to R side (6″ from L), close L FT to R. RPT and tap L FT on CT 4 as it closes R. REV L. (Emphasis must be placed on student staying in demi-plie, stepping on the flat FT and keeping FT apart. Opposition hip also added to this walk—push hip left as you step side-right.)	Arms are in low 2nd POS with jazz HNDS

HIP ISOLATION LEFT

FOUR CORNERS WALK

COUNTS	BODY MOVEMENT	ARM MOVEMENT
1-2	Step R FWD, tap L to C#2	Arms cross chest CT 1 and
3-4	Step L FWD, tap R to C#1	open to 2nd CT 2 (elbows
5-6	Step R FWD, tap L to C#3	flexed), clenched fists.
7-8	Step L FWD, tap R to C#4	Same
1-8	RPT adding identical hip with tap	
1-8	RPT adding pelvis circle and release (circle L, then R)	

TAP TO CORNER

JAZZ SQUARE

COUNTS	BODY MOVEMENT	ARM MOVEMENT
1-2	R FT crosses over L (hold 2)	L arm locked at elbow swings FRT, R arm 2nd POS
3-4	L FT steps BK (hold 4)	R makes a DWN swing and to middle of chest. L 2nd POS on the beat.
5-6	R FT steps to the side (hold 6)	V-POS OVRHD, R side
7-8	L FT steps FRT (hold 8)	Jazz HNDS, 2nd POS
	This square is also done with a catch step on CTS 7 and 8.	
	May also be done in 4 CTS, stepping on every beat.	

CROSS RIGHT
OVER LEFT

PELVIS LIFT — RIGHT AND LEFT

COUNTS	BODY MOVEMENT	ARM MOVEMENT
1-4	Face FRT, legs in plie. R hip and pelvis lifts for 4 CTS, as R toe taps the FLR for 3 CTS and step R FT on CT 4.	R arm is in 2nd POS with locked elbow — L HND & arm push FRT from SHL. CT 4 1st POS.
5-8	Reverse to L	Same as above with L arm in 2nd & R arm pushing FRT

PELVIS LIFT RIGHT

KNEE TWIST

COUNTS	BODY MOVEMENT	ARM MOVEMENT
1	Pique R FWD to C#1	Arms in 2nd
2	L in neutral passe, plie on R	R arm to SHL on CT 2
3	Releve on R STR FWD	R arm shoots OVRHD, jazz HND
4	Step L	R pulls DWN at elbow with
5-8	RPT	clenched fist
1-8	Walk BK (R, L, R, L)	

KNEE TWIST

AFRO JAZZ WALK

COUNTS	BODY MOVEMENT	ARM MOVEMENT
1	Both legs deep plie. Step R FT on place on CT 1. Body bent and chest parallel to FLR, BK STR, buttocks up, HD up and face FRT.	Arms bent and at sides
2	L FT reaches FRT with locked R knee (legs lock). Chest parallel to FLR for this combination.	R arm reaches FRT, elbow locked. L arm is bent at elbow and in BK of body.
3-8	RPT above	

AFRO WALK

"Beginners . . . forget that you are watching each other; don't try to make your movements pretty. We don't look for control in the beginning. First you find the river, then build the dam."

Sample Beginning Combination

Note: Done center floor

BEGINNING JAZZ COMBINATIONS

Beginning Jazz Combinations should be kept simple, with stress on clean technique and repetitions.

Include: Jazz Walks, Isolations, Levels, Port de Bras and Focus. Remember, start slowly, then progress to faster tempo.

SAMPLE:

Step I

COUNTS	BODY MOVEMENT	ARM MOVEMENT
1-4	FT 2nd POS, neutral, ISOL R knee TI on 1, lock 2, RPT	2nd POS, jazz HND
5	XROL — travel L	LJA
& 6	Hip lift R, focus S#8—step L, R	4th POS (L FWD, R 2nd)
7	Close L to R	Press to 1st POS
8	Step R to 2nd, neutral	LJA
1-8	RPT above	
1-16	Reverse and RPT L	
1-2	Releve, step R jazz WLK FWD	Thrust L jazz HND FWD, R jazz HND BK
3-4	Plie, step L jazz WLK FWD	Thrust R FWD, L BK
5-8	Change directions, RPT above (Sharp focus to S#8)	RPT all above
1-4	Change direction, RPT (Sharp focus to S#7)	Same
5-8	Change direction, RPT (Sharp focus to S#6)	Same

Step II

COUNTS	BODY MOVEMENT	ARM MOVEMENT
1-2	Face FRT — step R BK plie, step L to 2nd plie	Swing L jazz HND 2nd POS Swing R jazz HND 2nd POS
3-4	Step R FWD plie Batt L FWD, flex FT	LJA Jazz HND thrust 2nd
&5-8	RPT and reverse above	Same as above
1-8	RPT R & L above	

Step II—Continued

COUNTS	BODY MOVEMENT	ARM MOVEMENT
1 & 2	Chasse R, L, R to R side	R arm circles to 2nd, OVRHD, across torso
3-4	Step L BK to 4th, R FWD	R jazz HND 2nd — SHL ISOL R FWD & BK
5 & 6	Chasse, L, R, L to L side	L arm circles to 2nd, OVRHD, across torso
7-8	Step R BK to 4th L FWD	L jazz HND 2nd — SHL ISOL L FWD & BK
1-8	RPT above	
1-16	RPT, using both arms crossing and SHL ISOL R, L	

Repeat all from the very beginning of this combination. When you feel the group has technically perfected this combination, take a faster tempo, but make sure the clean technique still prevails.

Grade 2

Beginning II Jazz Class

Floor Stretches

Note: *See grade 1 for primary stretches used for all grades*

ISOLATION FLEX

LOF   Arms 2nd POS   Palms DWN
Legs STR   Toes PTD

COUNTS	BODY MOVEMENT	ARMS
1-2	Arch BK	2nd POS, palms DWN
3-4	Flex knees and ankles	
5-6	Hold	Lift palms (fingers to ceiling—wrist on FLR)
7-8	Lift HD	
1-2	Lock knees and ankles	
3-4	BK returns to FLR	
5-6	Hold	Return palms to FLR
7-8	Return HD to FLR	
1-48	RPT 3 Xs	
1-16	Above also done on beat (ISOL on every CT)	
1-2	Flex knees, FT, HNDS, HD, arch BK (All at same time)	
3-4	Return to FLR	
5-8	RPT	
1-24	RPT 3 Xs	

ISOLATION FLEX

VARIATION ON NEUTRAL KNEE PULSE
(Stretch for Vertebrae)

LOF   Arms 2nd POS   Palms DWN
Legs STR   Toes PTD

ARMS	BODY MOVEMENT	ARMS
1-2	R knee neutral passe	Both wrapped under FT
3-4	Lift HD to knee	Same
1-8	Hold POS	
1-8	Knee under chin — Hold	Same
1-8	Knee at ear — Hold	HNDS around FT
1-8	Knee at forehead — Hold	Open 2nd off FLR
1-4	Develope R to ceiling	Same
5-8	Lower leg and torso to FLR	
1-44	Reverse above to L knee	Same

KNEE TO FOREHEAD

PELVIS LIFT AND BODY ROLL

SOF   Jazz Split (R leg extended to C#1,
L leg flexed BK)

COUNTS	BODY MOVEMENT	ARMS
1	Sit in jazz split (R FWD, L BK)	R palm on FLR, L HND reaches to R toe
2	Hold	L arm bends and moves to chest
3	Lift pelvis off FLR	Lock R elbow, L arm reaches to ceiling
4	Return pelvis to FLR (sit)	L arm returns to chest
5-8	RPT	
1-8	RPT all above	
1-4	Body roll R-L leg attitude. End of stomach roll, place R leg attitude, straighten L leg DIAG	Place HNDS on FLR R
1-16	RPT all of exericse to L	

PELVIS LIFT

FRONT THIGH STRETCHES (Quadriceps Muscles)

SOF   Legs 1st POS   PT toes   Lean BK
Forearms and palms on FLR, back of pelvis

AHMS	BODY MOVEMENT	ARMS
1-2	Lift R leg to 90°, PT toe, knee locked	Same as above
3-4	Flex R ankle	
5-6	Bend from knee, PT toe	
7-8	Return to 90°, flex ankle	
1-8	RPT above	Same
1-4	Descend to FLR, flex ankle	
5-8	Pulse FWD from hip socket (over legs)	Above HD, V POS
1-24	Reverse to L	
1-24	RPT using both legs AST	

(Remember, lower BK Is STR during exercise.)

FORWARD BATTEMENT

SIT UPS COMBINATION

LOF   Knees locked   Toes PTD
Arms wrapped around rib cage

COUNTS	BODY MOVEMENT	ARMS
1-2 (Slow)	**Contract to square (sitting POS)**	**Wrapped around rib cage**
3-4	**Contract to FLR (pelvis, rib-cage)**	**Same**
5-16	**RPT 3 Xs**	
1-16	**RPT 16 CTS with flexed knees and ankles**	**Same**
1-16	**RPT above 16 CTS, locked knees, PTD toes**	**HNDS at nape of neck, elbow 2nd POS**
1-16	**RPT above 16 CTS with flexed knees and FT**	
1-32	**RPT all above**	**V POS OVRHD (arms remain in place OVRHD — do not swing through — use BK to raise from FLR)**

SIT UP CONTRACTION
ARMS AROUND RIB-CAGE

SIT UP CONTRACTION
ARMS AT NAPE OF NECK

CROSSED SWASTIKA STRETCH

SOF   RXL, HNDS   Hold ankle or FT

LEG TO CEILING STRETCH

COUNTS	BODY MOVEMENT	ARMS
1-4	**Stretch R leg NTO, to ceiling in line with R SHL**	**Hold ankles, elbows 2nd POS**
5-8	**Pulse TWD SHL**	
1-4	**Release HNDS, hold extension**	**Open 2nd LJA**
5-8	**Return RXL**	
1-4	**Stretch R leg to 2nd POS, TO, lock**	**R HND at instep of R FT, L 2nd, LJA**
5-8	**Pulse R leg 2nd**	
1-4	**Release HND, hold 2nd POS**	**2nd POS LJA (arm FWD of leg)**
5-8	**Return RXL**	
1-2	**Developpe R leg 2nd (off FLR), BK STR**	**2nd POS LJA (arms FWD of leg)**
3-4	**Developpe L leg 2nd (off FLR)**	**Same**
5-6	**Fold R leg in front (on FLR)**	
7-8	**Cross L over R (ready for L side), end in swastika POS**	
1-32	**REV and RPT above L**	
1-32	**RPT developpe changes L and R (4 Xs)**	**2nd POS LJA (arms FWD of leg)**

TABLETOP TO V POSITION

SOF   Bent knees together   FT 1st POS next
to buttocks   HD DWN   Arms around knees

COUNTS	BODY MOVEMENT	ARMS
1-4	Open to TBTP legs	2nd LJA
5-8	DEV to V POS sit	V POS OVRHD
1-8	Hold V POS	Same
1-4	RET to TBTP legs	Press to 2nd LJA
5-8	CON to LOF	JH, LJA
1-4 (Slow)	BATT, legs up, legs DWN to FLR (2 Xs)	2nd POS, palms on FLR
5-8	Open 2nd, close 1st (2 Xs)	
4-8's	RPT—roll up to TBTP POS and continue exercise	

V POSITION SIT

V POSITION TO SWASTIKA

LOF   Arms 2nd POS   Palms DWN
Legs STR   Toes PTD

COUNTS	BODY MOVEMENT	ARMS
1-2	Contract to TBTP legs	LJA 2nd POS
3-4	V POS sit	V POS OVRHD
5-8	Sit Swastika facing S#8 (R FRT, L BK)	Press to LJA 2nd
1-8	REV above 8 CTS	
1-16	RPT all above	

V POSITION SIT   SWASTIKA SIT

JAZZ SPLIT LIFT with FLOOR ROLL
(Changing right and left)

SOF   R leg extended to R DIAG
L leg flexed BK   Arm 2nd LJA

COUNTS	BODY MOVEMENT	ARMS
1 (Slow)	**Sit in jazz split**	**R palm on FLR, L arm reaches to R toe**
2	**L elbow into chest**	
3	**Lift pelvis, arch torso, lock R elbow**	**L arm reaches OVRHD**
4	**Sit**	**L elbow into chest**
5-6,7	**Roll R to stomach (L leg ATT CTS 5,6)**	**Both HNDS on FLR, R at SHL**
8	**Sit, flex R knee BK, extend L leg to L DIAG**	**2nd LJA**
1-8	**REV above 8 CTS**	
1-16	**RPT R and L**	

PELVIS LIFT

JAZZ SPLIT

STRETCH FOR UPPER INSIDE
THIGH MUSCLE OF LEGS

SOF   Legs 2nd POS   Toes PTD
Palms of HNDS on FLR BK of buttocks

COUNTS	BODY MOVEMENT	ARMS
1	**Lift pelvis off FLR, flex FT**	**Palms on FLR**
2	**Push pelvis FWD, PT toes**	
3	**Sit on FLR, toes PTD**	
4	**Readjust rib-cage, square POS**	

(This stretch is done until you have your maximum stretch in 2nd pos 180°. Keep HND on FLR in BK of you and use the FLR to pulse, keep pushing torso FWD.)

Keeping your legs in 2nd POS all of the time, remove HNDS from in BK of you and start your FWD reach— HNDS are reaching FWD on FLR. (Try to get your HD on FLR, then chest and then stomach muscles.)

Remember, legs must be TO from hip socket throughout stretch. Exercise is done pulsing very slowly.

Dancer must strive for 180° opening in 2nd POS.

SECOND POSITION STRETCH

MAXIMUM SECOND POSITION EXTENSION STRETCH

SOF   Legs in 2nd POS, TO, pushing through the small
part of the BK with the head up. (Exercise done
only after 180° warmup with legs in 2nd POS.)

COUNTS	BODY MOVEMENT	ARMS
1-16	Bounce FWD, BK STR	Palms on FLR, push elbows to FLR
1-8	Walk HNDS FWD	
1-8	Hold — Do not pulse (holding strengthens muscles and tendons)	
1-96	RPT entire stretch 3 Xs	

MAXIMUM SECOND STRETCH

POINT AND FLEX FEET

SOF   Legs 2nd POS, TO   Arms 2nd POS, LJA

COUNTS	BODY MOVEMENT	ARMS
1 (Slow)	PT R toe	2nd LJA
2	Flex toe and flex knee	
3-4	RPT L (STR R)	
5-6	RPT, alternating R and L	
7-8	RPT both at the same time	
1-24	RPT 3 Xs	

FLEX ANKLE AND KNEE

SIDE STRETCH AND TABLETOP BACK

Kneel on L knee   R leg is in 2nd   Arms 2nd ILJA

COUNTS	BODY MOVEMENT	ARMS
1-4	Stretch to R side	Arms OVRHD, V POS
5-8	Bend FWD, chest parallel to FLR, TBTP	Arms 2nd POS
1-8	Contract, placing HD on FLR	Interlace fingers, small of BK, reach FWD, pulsing
1-4	Scoop up to starting POS	V POS OVRHD
5-8	Close R knee to L	1st POS
1-72	RPT exercises 3 Xs	
1-96	REV and RPT exercise to L side	Same as above

SIDE STRETCH

CONTRACTIONS TO FLOOR FROM LUNGE POSITION

Kneeling on both knees
Arms at sides (square POS)

COUNTS	BODY MOVEMENT	ARMS
1-2	Lunge FWD R, NTO	LJA 2nd POS
3-4	Return to both knees	Arms DWN 1st
5-6	Lunge R 2nd POS	LJA 2nd POS
7-8	Contract to FLR, sit on FLR (accent pelvis under)	JH 2nd POS
1-4	Hold	LJA 2nd POS
5-8	Contract pelvis to kneeling POS (L knee on FLR, R FT 2nd lunge)	JH 2nd POS
1-2	Stretch to 2nd (Pulse R lunge)	LJA
3-4	Return to both knees	Same
5-8	Hold	Press to 1st
3-8's	REV and RPT L	
	Exercise also done on beat.	

LUNGE FORWARD   LUNGE SECOND   CONTRACT AND SIT ON FLOOR

KNEE HINGE—Stretch for strengthening quadriceps muscles (front of upper thigh)

Kneel on both knees, 2nd POS, square
Arms 2nd, LJA

45° KNEE HINGE

COUNTS	BODY MOVEMENT	ARMS
1-4	Lie BK with pelvis locked (knee hinge) 45°	2nd LJA
5-8	Lift to upright kneeling POS	
1-4	Lean BK far as you can without releasing the pelvis (arch BK, place top of HD on FLR)	V POS OVRHD (palms PP)
5-8	Arch to upright kneeling POS	
1-8	Sit pelvis on FLR, between FT	1st POS
1-72	Exercise done slowly — RPT 3 Xs	

USING ARMS WITH CONTRACTION AND RELEASE OF RIB-CAGE, PELVIS AND HEAD

CB   4th POS, TO, R FT FWD on toe
Standing POS   Both legs demi-plie   Face C#1

COUNTS	ARMS
1-4	Bring arms to V POS from SHLS (lead with wrists and inside part of arm, elbows locked, HNDS trail)
5-8	Open arms to 2nd—elbows lead, palms PP to FLR
1-4	Bring arms together contracting rib-cage only
5-8	Open arms to 2nd neutral rib-cage
1-4	Bring arms together contracting rib-cage and pelvis
5-8	Open arms to 2nd neutral rib-cage and pelvis
1-4	Bring arms together contracting rib-cage, pelvis and head
5-8	Open arms to 2nd neutral rib-cage, pelvis, and HD
	Done 4 Xs, then reverse to L side, face C#2, L FT FWD, toe PTD
	Same exercise is also done diminishing to lesser CTS—2 CTS FWD, 2 CTS BK
	Same exercise done releasing rib-cage, rib-cage and pelvis, rib-cage, pelvis and HD. Start arms V POS FRT of chest (palms out, wrists press to 2nd POS and return to V FWD)
	Same exercise done moving from CON to REL without stop at neutral (wrists in on CON, wrists out on REL and move to 2nd)

RIB-CAGE AND
PELVIS CONTRACTION

"Don't close your eyes; always keep them open and with sharp focus."

DIAGONAL ARM STRETCH AND LUNGE EXERCISE

CB   FT 2nd POS, TO   Standing POS   Arms 1st POS

COUNTS	BODY MOVEMENT	ARMS
1-4	Step R 2nd POS, ISOL R knee TI, L knee remains locked.	R arm reaches OVRHD and to 2nd, L HND on pelvis
5-8	Torso twists to S#6, HD looks over R SHL, lunge L.	R arm moves to C#2, L to C#4. Arms are now in DIAG POS
1-8	Lunge with L knee to S#6, grande-plie. R leg is locked and FT is flexed. Pulse heel and hip of R leg to FLR.	Place HNDS on knee
1-8	TBTP lunge, chest parallel to FLR, PT toe, place weight on instep. Continue pulse.	Arms parallel to FLR, V POS OVRHD
1-4	Lift torso to 2nd POS, grande-plie facing FWD. Keep pulsing in 2nd POS.	Arms 2nd POS, jazz HNDS
5-8	Return to standing POS	Arms press to 1st
1-32	REV and RPT L	
1-64	RPT all above R and L	Same

KNEE TURNED-IN   TABLETOP LUNGE

PLIE, TENDU, BATTEMENT EXERCISE

CB   5th POS, TO   R FT FRT   Arms at sides

COUNTS	BODY MOVEMENT	ARMS
1-2	Plie	Arms move to 2nd POS, LJA
3	Tendu front, R FT	
4	Releve supporting FT ("plie-releve" POS)	Same
5	Battement FWD, R leg	
6	PT R on FLR, 4th	
7	Lower heel and lock knee of L leg	
&	Bring R FT in front to passe TO POS, locking supporting knee	
8	Take R FT to BK passe POS	
&	Close R FT to 5th in BK	
1-8	Reverse to L side	
	Exercise done 4 Xs each side	
	Also done with tendu 2nd POS	
	Also done arabesque POS BK	

FORWARD TENDU

FEET AND ARMS — COORDINATION

CB   FT PP 1st   Arms 1st

COUNTS	BODY MOVEMENT	ARMS
1	Step R 2nd POS TO, lock	R jazz HND 2nd
2	Step L 2nd POS TO, lock	L jazz HND 2nd
3	Demi-plie 2nd POS TO	Palms FRT of chest, elbows out 2nd
4	Jump to 1st PP, knees locked	Jazz HNDS 2nd POS
5	Step R 2nd POS TI	BK of R jazz HND 2nd
6	Step L 2nd POS TI	BK of L jazz HND 2nd
7	Plie 2nd POS TI	Palms FRT of chest, elbows out 2nd
8	Jump to 1st PP, knees locked	1st POS
1-8	RPT start L step to 2nd TO	Same
1-16	RPT R and L	Same
	Also done "plie-releve" POS with heel off FLR, demi-plie	

FEET TURNED OUT   FEET TURNED-IN

GRANDE PLIE COMBINATION

5th POS TO   R FT FRT   Arms 1st POS

COUNTS	BODY MOVEMENT	ARMS
1,2,3 (Slow)	**Brush R FWD attitude, TO. Extend R leg CT 2, flex R ankle CT 3.**	**2nd POS LJA**
4	**Step R 4th POS FWD TO**	**1st POS**
5-8	**Grande plie 4th POS**	**Lift to 2nd POS LJA**
9-12	**Lift to locked knees**	**Press DWN to 1st**
1,2,3	**Brush R 2nd attitude. Extend R leg CT 2, flex R ankle CT 3.**	**2nd POS LJA — arms FRT of leg**
4	**Step R 2nd POS TO**	**Same**
5-8	**Grande plie 2nd POS**	**Circle OVRHD and to 2nd LJA**
9-12	**Lift to locked knees**	**Press DWN to 1st**
1,2,3	**Brush R BK attitude**	**4th POS (R FWD OVRHD jazz HND, L 2nd POS)**
4	**Step R 4th POS BK**	**Same**
5-8	**Grande plie 4th POS**	**L swings OVRHD, PP pull DWN from elbows**
9-12	**Lift to locked knees**	**Open to 2nd POS LJA on 9, 10. Press to 1st on 11, 12.**
1-8	**Step R 2nd, L BK to 4th. Sit to FLR in crossed swastika POS (BK STR)**	**Circle into chest out to 2nd jazz HNDS**
9-12	**Lift to standing POS, FT PP 1st**	**Lift to 2nd LJA and press to 1st**
6, 8's	**RPT and REV, brush L FWD attitude**	

FRONT ATTITUDE
TURNED-OUT

GRANDE PLIE
2nd POSITION

PARALLEL PULL DOWN
FROM ELBOWS

FEET — SOUS-SUS PROGRESSION
(Back, forward and diagonal)

CB   1st POS NTO   Arms 1st

COUNTS	BODY MOVEMENT	ARMS
&1	Step BK R plie, close L releve 5th (Sous-sus) L FRT	2nd LJA
2	Step R FRT, plie	2nd jazz HNDS
&3	Step BK L, R releve 5th, R FRT	2nd LJA
4	Step L FRT	2nd jazz HNDS
&5	Step FWD R, L releve 5th, L BK	2nd LJA
6	Step R BK, plie	2nd jazz HNDS
&7	Step FWD L, R releve 5th, R BK	2nd LJA
8	Step L BK, plie	2nd jazz HNDS
&1-4	Sous-sus also done on L and R DIAG (face C2 then C1)	Arms as above
&5-8	RPT DIAG sous-sus	(Opposite arm may circle 2nd, OVRHD and into chest and FWD on DIAG, on CTS 2 & 4)
1-16	RPT entire exercise above	

SOUS-SUS

PERCUSSIVE ISOLATION PROGRESSION
—Head, Shoulders, Rib-Cage, and Pelvis

CB   FT 2nd PP   Arms 1st POS (All isolations done with a percussive accent, in 8 count phrases. Hit ISOL on each count.)

COUNTS	MOVEMENT
1-8 (Slow)	HD—FWD thrust (8 Xs) — return to neutral CT 2
1-8	HD—BK thrust
1-8	HD—R side
1-8	HD—L side
1-8	HD—R side tilt
1-8	HD—L side tilt
1-8	HD—square (thrust FRT, R, BK, L — RPT)
1-8	HD—square (thrust FRT, L, etc.)
1-8	HD—vertical (like yes), chin DWN on beat
1-8	HD—horizontal (like no)
1-8	HD—lateral (tilting R and L)

PERCUSSIVE ISOLATION PROGRESSION—Continued

1-8	HD—swings (L to R and R to L)
1-8	HD—swing and circle (swing R and L and circle R)
1-8	HD—swing and circle (swing L and R and circle L)
1-16	Relax—bend at waist and let HD hang to FLR, CON and up
1-8	R SHL—FWD hit — return to neutral CT 2
1-8	L SHL—FWD hit
1-8	R SHL—BK hit
1-8	L SHL—BK hit
1-8	R SHL—lift up
1-8	L SHL—lift up
1-8	R SHL—push DWN
1-8	L SHL—push DWN
1-8	R SHL—circle BK
1-8	L SHL—circle BK
1-8	R SHL—circle FWD
1-8	L SHL—circle FWD
1-8	R SHL—R arm to C#1, palm DWN, pull arm BK from SHL
1-8	L SHL—L arm to C#2, palm DWN, pull arm BK from SHL
1-16	Relax—bend FWD at waist and let SHL and HD relax, CON and up
1-8	Rib-cage—isolate to R side — return to neutral CT 2
1-8	Rib-cage—isolate to L side
1-8	Rib-cage—release (FWD)
1-8	Rib-cage—CON (BK)
1-8	Rib-cage square—R, FRT, L, BK, RPT
1-8	Rib-cage square L
1-8	Rib-cage figure 8 (R and L)
1-8	Rib-cage figure 8 (L and R)
1-16	Relax—bend FWD at waist and let torso hang, CON and up
1-8	Pelvis hits R, FT 2nd PP, demi-plie, arms jazz HND 2nd
1-8	Pelvis hits L
1-8	Pelvis release (hits BK)
1-8	Pelvis CON (hits FWD)
1-8	Pelvis square R (R, FRT, L, BK, RPT)
1-8	Pelvis square L (L, FRT, R, BK, RPT)
1-8	Pelvis figure 8 (R and L)
1-8	Pelvis figure 8 (L and R)
1-16	Relax and bend FWD from waist, CON and up

HEAD FORWARD THRUST

HEAD BACK THRUST

HEAD SIDE ISOLATION

HEAD SIDE TILT

SHOULDER ISOLATION
FORWARD

SHOULDER ISOLATION
UP

SHOULDER ISOLATION
DOWN

SHOULDER ISOLATION
PULL BACK

FORWARD BEND AND RELAX

RIB-CAGE ISOLATION—SIDE

PELVIS ISOLATION—SIDE

"Ligaments lose their elasticity with lack of use."

FEET—Flex, Point Exercise

CB   1st PP   Arms 1st

COUNTS	BODY MOVEMENT	ARMS
1-8	PT R FWD, flex R ankle, RPT and close 1st CT 8 (NTO on FLR)	2nd POS LJA
1-8	REV and RPT L	Same
1-8	2nd POS TO, R PT, flex	Same
1-8	2nd POS TO, L PT, flex	Same
1-8	Arabesque (R BK), PT-flex TO	Same
1-8	Arabesque (L BK), PT-flex TO	Same
	RPT entire exercise with working leg at knee height	
	RPT entire exercise with working leg at hip height (if class is ready)	

FLEX ANKLE

FEET—Turned In, Turned Out from Hip Socket

CB   FT PP 1st   Arms 1st

COUNTS	BODY MOVEMENT	ARMS
1 (Slow)	Step R 2nd PP, locked knee	Jazz HNDS 2nd POS
2	Step R TO to C#1, locked knee	4th POS L FWD
3	Step R 2nd PP (face FRT), locked	Jazz HNDS 2nd POS
4	Step R 2nd PP TI, locked	Thrust jazz HNDS to C#2
5	Close R to L PP 1st, locked	1st
6	Step R FWD TI, ISOL R SHL FRT, locked	4th POS (L FWD, R 2nd)
7	Releve 1st POS PP	Jazz HNDS 2nd POS
&8	Demi-plie	Press to 1st POS
1-8	RPT and REV L (step L 2nd PP)	
1-16	RPT entire combination R and L	
	Also done with plie on working leg	
	May also be done with releve heel on the working leg	

TURNED-OUT LUNGE

TURNED-IN FORWARD

FEET—Passe Exercise Turned Out

CB   5th POS   R FRT   Arms 1st

COUNTS	BODY MOVEMENT	ARMS
&1 (Slow)	**Passe R close 5th POS BK, ankle height (toes must PT)**	**2nd POS LJA**
&2	**Passe R close 5th POS FRT**	**Same**
&3, &8	**RPT above**	**Same**
&1, &8	**Passe L FRT BK, ankle height**	**Same**
&1, &8	**Passe R, knee height (CHK PTD toes)**	**Same**
&1, &8	**Passe L, knee height**	**Same**
&4-8's	**RPT all above adding plie on "&" CT**	**Same**
1-16	**End with pique balance (L toe at knee TO)**	**V POS OVRHD**
1-16	**Change pique balance (R toe at knee TO) (plie CTS 15, 16, 5th POS R FRT)**	**Same**
	RPT entire exercise	

PASSE POSITION   PIQUE POSITION

FEET—Tendu (stretch for instep)

CB   5th POS R BK   Arms 1st

COUNTS	BODY MOVEMENT	ARMS
1-2	**Brush and PT R toes 2nd TO (press heel FWD). Close R 5th POS FRT (travel FWD).**	**2nd POS LJA**
3-4	**Brush and PT L toes 2nd TO. Close L 5th POS FRT.**	**Same**
5-8	**RPT R and L above**	**Same**
1-8	**Start L Tendu (travel BK)**	**Same**
1-16	**RPT R and L above**	
	Tendus may be done with plie CT 1, also done with plie, releve CTS 1, 2.	
	Also done with degage (brushing toes off FLR), knee height, then waist height.	

2nd POSITION TENDU

LEG SWINGS—Attitude Back, Front

CB   Standing on L, R BK attitude   Arms 2nd LJA

COUNTS	BODY MOVEMENT	ARMS
1-6	Brush R attitude FRT, BK RPT to 6th CT	LJA
7	Releve L, FRT attitude R	Same
8	Step R FRT, BK attitude L	Same
1-8	RPT and REV L attitude	Same
1-16	RPT R and L above	
1-8	Diminish to 4 CTS (releve 3 and 7)	Same
1-8	RPT 4 CT attitudes	
1-8	Diminish to 2 CTS (releve 1, 3, 5, 7)	Same
	Exercise may also be done with HD snapping R and L sides on releve CTS.	
	Exercise also done 2nd and across body POS leg swing, CT 8, 2nd POS grande-plie.	

FRONT ATTITUDE

LEGS—Flex Battement Forward, Second, Back

CB   4th POS NTO   R FT BK   Arms 1st POS

COUNTS	BODY MOVEMENT	ARMS
&1 (Slow)	Plie L, battement R FWD, flex ankle (lock L on CT 1), torso FRT	Jazz HNDS 2nd POS
&2	Passe R, TO, plie L, battement R 2nd flex ankle (lock L on CT 2)	LJA 2nd POS
&3	Passe R, TO, plie L, battement R BK, flex ankle (lock L on CT 3)	V POS OVRHD
&4	Turn in R knee 2nd POS	4th POS (L FRT, R 2nd)
5	Step R PP 2nd	1st
6	Release HD and pelvis, grande-plie	Same
7	CON HD and pelvis, lift to locked knees	Same
8	Step L BK, 4th POS	Same
1-8	RPT and REV plie R, battement L	
1-16	RPT all above R and L	
	Exercise also done plie, releve, or "plie-releve" POS, CT 1	

FORWARD BATTEMENT,
FLEX ANKLE

TORSO—Release and Contract Coordination

CB   1st POS NTO   Arms 1st

COUNTS	BODY MOVEMENT	ARMS
1,2 (Slow)	Step R 2nd, NTO, demi-plie	2nd POS LJA
3-4	CON rib-cage	Jazz HNDS press FWD, 2nd
5-6	Release pelvis and HD, grande-plie 2nd POS	1st
7&8	CON pelvis and rib-cage , HD and lift to locked knees, close R to L, PP 1st, CT 8	1st
1-8	RPT and REV, step L 2nd	Same
1-16	RPT all above, R and L	
	Diminish to 4 CTS and take each movement on the beat.	

2nd POSITION PARALLEL,
DEMI-PLIE —
CONTRACT RIB-CAGE

LEGS—Developpe Forward, Second and Arabesque

CB   5th POS TO, R FT FRT   Arms 1st

COUNTS	BODY MOVEMENT	ARMS
1	Plie L, coupe R FRT (PTD toes at ankle)	2nd POS LJA
2-4	Developpe R FRT to full extension, PT, lock L knee	Same
5	Plie L, coupe R FRT	Same
6-8	Developpe R 2nd to full extension, PT, lock L knee	Same
1	Plie L, coupe R BK	Same
2-4	Developpe R BK to arabesque	Same
5-6	Demi-plie, 5th POS TO, R FT BK	1st
7-8	Lock knees, 5th POS	Same
1-16	RPT and REV, coupe L FRT	
	May also be done with plie, releve or "plie-releve" POS	

COUPE

DEVELOPPE—RIGHT FRONT

ARABESQUE

LEGS—Developpe-Releve

CB   5th POS TO   R FT BK   Arms 1st POS

COUNTS	BODY MOVEMENT	ARMS
1-2	Step BK R plie, TO	2nd POS LJA
3-4	Developpe L FWD, "plie-releve"	Same
5-6	Releve R, hold L extended FRT	Same
7-8	Rock and step L FWD, R BK	Thrust jazz HNDS FWD CT 7, 1st on CT 8
1-8	RPT and REV, step BK L	
1-16	RPT R and L	

Exercise also done with develope to 2nd POS (CTS 7, 8 remain same). May also be done in arabesque (BK) position.

DEVELOPPE– "PLIE-RELEVE"
SUPPORTING LEG

ISOLATION COORDINATION

CB   FT 1st POS PP   Arms 1st

COUNTS	BODY MOVEMENT	ARMS
1	Step R 2nd PP plie, ISOL L hip	Palms FRT of chest, elbows out 2nd
2	Tap L BK 4th POS, lock	Thrust R jazz HND OVRHD, L holds at chest
3	Hold and ISOL L SHL, plie	Circle R arm to 2nd, jazz HND — L holds
4	Bend to L side, ISOL R SHL	Fan L arm L, fan R to chest
5-6	Tap L 2nd POS, step L DIAG BK C#3, ISOL L hip and L SHL	Circle L to SHL and push palm 2nd
7-8	RPT and REV above (Tap R)	Same
1-8	RPT entire combination above (step L 2nd)	
1-16	RPT combination R and L	

LEFT HIP ISOLATION

RIGHT ARM
SIDE STRETCH

Jazz Walk Combinations

JAZZ WALKS DONE IN SERIES OF 8 CT PROGRESSIONS FORWARD AND BACKWARD
(Repeat each walk.)

COUNTS	BODY MOVEMENT	ARMS

BOUNCE WALK

1	Step FWD R	Arms swing naturally (L FWD)
2	Plie on R with L in neutral passe	
3-8	RPT to L, R, L (8 CTS FWD and 8 CTS BK)	R FWD (then L and R)

TAP STEP

1	Tap R toe FWD, NTO, lock L	Arms swing naturally
2	Step R FWD plie	
3-8	RPT to L (8 CTS FWD and 8 CTS BK)	
	Also done in releve and with HD thrust FWD on CT 1 and BK to neutral on CT 2.	

TAP STEP WITH CONTRACTION AND RELEASE OF RIB-CAGE

1-2	FT same as above. Rib-cage contracts on CT 1 and releases on CT 2	Arms cross in FRT of chest, elbows bent on CT 1; on CT 2
3-8	RPT to L, R, L	arms open to 2nd POS leading with elbows, LJA
1-8	Walk BK (R, L, R, L)	

JAZZ WALK—FRONT WITH CATCH STEP

1&2 3&4 5&6 7&8	1) Step R foot FRT (same as above). Take a catch step on CTS &2 (catch step, two quick steps, in this case a quick LR— also called ball change in tap). REV com- bination by starting on L FT. RPT R & L.	X at chest and 2nd LJA

PASSE STEP BACK
(Backward Walk)

1	Passe R (releve) NTO	Arms 2nd POS, LJA
&2	Extend R leg to BK and step BK (plie)	
3&4	REV to L	
5-8	RPT	

WRIST ISOLATION WALKS

1-2	Step R FWD, NTO, plie	L wrist moves FWD in low POS (fingers trail)
3-4	RPT to L	L wrist moves BK
5-8	RPT R and L	
1-8	RPT walk BK (on CTS 7, 8, step L, R)	Same
1-16	Start L FT FWD (on last 2 CTS step R, L)	R wrist
1-16	RPT walks FWD and BK—start R (on last 2 CTS, step L, R)	L wrist leads arm up to SHL height and DWN
1-16	RPT walks FWD and BK—start L (on last 2 CTS, step R, L)	R wrist leads to SHL height and DWN
1-16	RPT walks—start R (on last 2 CTS, step L, R)	L wrist circles OVRHD (circles in, out)
1-16	RPT walks—start L (on last 2 CTS, step L, R)	R wrist circles OVRHD (circles in, out)
1-16	RPT walks—start R (add opp SHL — L SHL, R FT)	Both wrists circle OVRHD (circles in, out)

SPIDER WALK

1-8	2 CT walk (R,L,R,L) (as R steps FWD, L is in BK attitude — reverse)	2nd POS, jazz HND, roll HNDS and opposite SHLS FWD on CTS 2, 4, 6, 8
1-8	Jazz WLK BK	1st POS
1-16	RPT spider walk	Same as above

FUNKY WALK

&1	Plie L, step R FWD on CT 1, REL pelvis	Cross arms FRT of chest
&2	Tap L 2nd plie R	HNDS swing out next to SHLS
&3-8	REV and RPT	Same
1-8	RPT moving BK	

PELVIS LIFT—RIGHT AND LEFT

1-4	Face FRT, plie, R hip and pelvis lifts for 4 CTS, as R toe taps FLR for 3 CTS, step R FT CT 4.	Lift to high 4th, L FRT, R 2nd
5-8	REV to L	R FRT, L 2nd
1-8	RPT all above	

"People with poor circulation often get arthritis."

KNEE TWIST

1	Pique R FWD to C#1 (step R on ½ toe)	Arms in 2nd, LJA
2	L in neutral passe, plie on R	R arm to SHL on CT 2, L 2nd
3	Releve on R STR FWD	R arm shoots OVRHD, jazz HND
4	Step L FWD, plie	R pulls DWN at elbow with clenched fist
5-8	RPT	
1-8	Walk BK (R,L,R,L)	
1-8	RPT WLK FWD	
	Also may be done L	

FOUR CORNERS WALK

1-2	Step R FWD, tap L to C#2, HD looks to COR	Arms cross chest CT 1 and open to 2nd CT 2 (elbows flexed — fists)
3-4	Step L FWD, tap R to C#1	
5-6	Step R FWD, tap L to C#3	
7-8	Step L FWD, tap R to C#4	Same
1-8	RPT	
	Also may be done with pelvis and arms circle direction of tap.	

NEUTRAL POSITION PASSE—JAZZ WALK

R FT PTD BK   Arms 1st

COUNTS	BODY MOVEMENT	ARM MOVEMENT
1-2	Walk R-L FWD, NTO, plie	LJA 2nd
3-4	Walk R-L BK, NTO, plie	ILJA 2nd
5-6-7	R low passe POS, NTO, releve AST stretch torso to R side	High 4th (L OVRHD, R 2nd)
8	Step R FWD, CON pelvis	Jazz HNDS, 2nd POS
1-8	REV L	Same
1-16	RPT R and L	

TORSO STRETCH AND PASSE

LUNGE AND OUTSIDE TURN—JAZZ WALK

FT 1st POS, NTO, plie   Arms 1st

COUNTS	BODY MOVEMENT	ARM MOVEMENT
1-2	Walk R-L FWD, releve	LJA 2nd
3	Lunge R FWD, NTO	4th POS (L FWD, R 2nd)
4-5	Pivot ½ turn L, 2nd grande-plie, face S#7	2nd POS JH
6	Lunge L to S#7	4th POS (R FWD, L 2nd)
7&	OTR ½ or 1½ to face FRT (R passe NTO)	At chest
8	Step R FWD (face FRT)	4th POS (L FWD, R 2nd)
1-8	REV L	
1-16	RPT all above	

PIVOT—2nd GRANDE PLIE

JAZZ HAND AND SHOULDER ISOLATION —JAZZ WALK

FT 2nd POS, TO   L Arm V POS OVRHD   R 1st

COUNTS	BODY MOVEMENT	ARM MOVEMENT
1-2	Step R FWD, plie on CT 2	Push L palm FWD & DWN 2 CTS, R arm at side
3-4	REV L	REV — R reaches FWD
5	Step R 2nd NTO, plie	1st POS
6	Hold — ISOL L SHL FWD	R JH 2nd
7	FT TG plie, NTO	1st POS
8	Releve 1st POS NTO, ISOL R SHL FWD	L JH 2nd
1-8	REV	
1-16	RPT all above	

ISOLATION—LEFT SHOULDER FORWARD

HIGH HIP LIFT AND OUTSIDE TURN—JAZZ WALK

FT 1st POS, NTO, plie   Arms 1st

COUNTS	BODY MOVEMENT	ARM MOVEMENT
1&2	High hip lift R, step R facing S#6, torso twist	4th POS FWD, L FRT, R 2nd
&3	Step L-R FWD 4th POS (face S#6)	Same
&4	OTL, step L FWD, NTO, plie	At chest & TO 1st
5-6	Walk BK R-L, NTO, plie	DWN 1st POS
7&8	Step BK R-L, releve, FWD R, plie	ILJA on CT 8
1-8	REV	
1-16	RPT all above	HIGH HIP LIFT

PELVIS FIGURE 8 ROTATION—JAZZ WALK

Tap R Toe FWD, L leg plie   Arms LJA

COUNTS	BODY MOVEMENT	ARM MOVEMENT
1&2	Step R, L, R FWD, TI (face #6), plie	Push L wrist FWD 2, R on pelvis
3&4&	Rotate pelvis Fig. 8 (circle L & C & R, and circle R & CTR)	Same
5-8	REV	
1-8	RPT all above	

TURNED-IN RIGHT

BATTEMENT ON PLIE-RELEVE LEG—JAZZ WALK

Face C#2   PT R toe BK   Arms 2nd LJA

COUNTS	BODY MOVEMENT	ARM MOVEMENT
1-2	DIAG, walk FWD R-L TO, C2, plie	Cross at chest
3	Battement R croise, "plie-releve" L, torso and HD FWD	Stretch to DIAG, L FWD
4	Step FWD R	1st
5-8	REV L C1	
1-8	RPT all above (travel X FLR)	

BATTEMENT RIGHT CROISE

DEVELOPPE KICK FORWARD, PLIE-RELEVE SUPPORTING LEG—JAZZ WALK

R toe PTD BK   Arms 1st POS

COUNTS	BODY MOVEMENT	ARM MOVEMENT
1	Step R FWD, plie, NTO	DWN
&2	L-R FWD, "plie-releve" POS (face C#2)	LJA 2nd
&3	L-R BK, "plie-releve" POS (face C#2)	LJA 2nd
&4	DEV kick L FWD AST arch BK — supporting R leg "plie-releve"	4th
5-8	RPT and REV — step L FWD	
1-8	RPT above	

DEVELOPE KICK—
ARCH BACK

LAY OUT BACK ON "PLIE-RELEVE" SUPPORTING LEG —JAZZ WALK

Face C#1, R toe BK   Arms 2nd POS LJA

COUNTS	BODY MOVEMENT	ARM MOVEMENT
1	Step R C#1, plie	Cross FRT of chest
2	Battement L croise, "plie-releve" R	2nd LJA
3	Lay-out BK AST hold battement— "plie-releve" supporting leg	DIAG stretch
&4	Catch step L-R FWD, plie	1st POS
5-8	REV L	
1-8	RPT above	
1-16	RPT R and L traveling X FLR	

BATTEMENT LEFT
AND LAY-OUT

GRANDE PLIE 4th POSITION—JAZZ WALK

1st POS   Locked knees   Arms 2nd POS

COUNTS	BODY MOVEMENT	ARM MOVEMENT
1-2	Walk R-L FWD, NTO, plie	DWN
3	Deep plie 4th POS, R FWD ("plie-releve")	4th POS—L FRT, R 2nd
4	Releve 1st POS, NTO	ILJA 2nd
5-8	REV	Same
1-8	RPT above	
1-16	RPT R and L traveling X FLR	

DEEP PLIE—
4th POSITION

LEG FAN, OUTSIDE TURN AND SOUS-SUS—JAZZ WALK

FT 2nd POS, TO   Locked knee   Arms V POS FRT

COUNTS	BODY MOVEMENT	ARM MOVEMENT
1-2	Walk R-L FWD to C#2, plie	LJA 2nd
3-4	R leg circle (fan L to R), releve L, end 2nd POS plie	
5-6	Walk L-R FWD, plie	4th POS, L FRT, R 2nd
7&8	OTL end Sous-Sus, L FRT (face FRT)	2nd, jazz HNDS
1-8	REV L	
1-16	RPT R and L above	

FAN CIRCLE

MULTIPLES—JAZZ WALKS
A Study of Quick Movements for the Feet

TRIPLES   3 steps to 2 counts of music.
               Triples alternate from R FT to L FT
               Sample CTS: 3 & 4

QUADS   4 steps to 2 counts of music.
               Quads do not alternate; they remain on the same side.
               Sample CTS: 3 & a 4

QUINTS   5 steps to 2 counts of music.
               Quints alternate from R FT to L FT.
               Sample CTS: a 3 & a 4

FEET MULTIPLES

FT 1st PP, lock   Arms 1st

COUNTS	BODY MOVEMENT	ARM MOVEMENT
	TRIPLES ON PLACE (Alternating)	
1-2	Step R, L NTO plie, on place	Arms swing FWD, opposition
3&4	Step R, L 2nd releve, step R FWD plie	2nd & DWN 1st CT 4
5-8	REV above L	
1-8	RPT all above	
	TRIPLES TURNING	
1-2	Step R, L FWD, NTO, plie	Arms opposition
3&4	Turn R (step R, L releve, step R FWD plie)	2nd & DWN 1st CT 4
5-8	REV above L	
1-8	RPT all above	
	TRIPLES CHANGING HEAD DIRECTION	
1-2	Step R, L FWD, NTO, plie	Arms opposition
3&4	Step R, L, R releve 2nd POS. HD spots R, L, R	1st POS
5-8	REV above L	
1-8	RPT all above	
	TRIPLES MOVING BACK	
1-2	Walk BK R, L NTO, plie	1st POS
3&4	Triple BK R, L, R releve	Same
5-8	REV above L	Same

QUADS ON PLACE (Non-alternating)

1-2	Step R, L NTO plie, on place	Arms opposition
3 & a 4	Step R, L, R, L releve 2nd	2nd & DWN 1st CT 4
5-8	RPT above	Same
1-8	RPT all above	Same

QUADS TURNING

1-2	Step R, L FWD, NTO, plie	Arms opposition
3 & a 4	Turn R (step R, L, R releve, step L FWD plie CT 4	1st POS
5-8	RPT above	
1-8	RPT 1-8 above	Same

QUADS CHANGING HEAD DIRECTIONS

1-2	Step R, L FWD, NTO, plie	Arms opposition
3 & a 4	Step R, L, R, L releve 2nd POS HD spots R, L, R, L	1st POS
5-8	RPT above	
1-8	RPT 1-8 above	Same

QUADS MOVING BACK

1-2	WLK BK R, L, NTO, plie	1st POS
3 & a 4	Quad BK R, L, R, L releve	Same
5-8	RPT above	Same

QUINTS ON PLACE (Alternating)

1-2	Step R, L NTO, plie, on place	Arms opposition
a 3 & a 4	Step R, L, R, L 2nd releve, Step R FWD plie	2nd POS (a 3 &) Cross FRT of chest (a) DIAG L FRT (CT 4)
5-8	REV above L	Same
1-8	RPT all above	

QUINTS TURNING

1-2	Step R, L NTO FWD, plie	Arms opposition
a 3 & a 4	Turn R (step R, L, R, L releve Step R FWD plie)	1st POS
5-8	REV and RPT above L	Same
1-8	RPT all above	Same

QUINTS CHANGING HEAD DIRECTIONS

1-2	Step R, L, FWD, NTO, plie	Arms opposition
a 3 & a 4	Step R, L, R, L, R, releve 2nd POS HD spots R, L, R, L, R	1st POS
5-8	REV above L	Same
1-8	RPT all above	Same

QUINTS MOVING BACK

1-2	Walk BK R, L, NTO, plie	1st POS
a 3 & a 4	Quint BK R, L, R, L, R releve	Same
5-8	REV above L	Same

Triples, Quads and Quints may also be done traveling diagonally across floor, or in large circle (using diagonal arms, ending opposite of foot that is forward).

Multiples are also effective when using a strong sustained movement before and after the multiple.

Example:

COUNTS	BODY MOVEMENT	ARM MOVEMENT
1-2	R high hip lift, torso twist, step R plie CT 2	R jazz HND OVRHD CT 1 Pull elbow to R side CT 2
3	Hold POS—HD looks L	Hold
4	Hold	Circle R to SHL and 2nd
a 5 & a 6	Quint—Step R FWD, plie Step L BK, plie Step R 2nd, releve Step L 2nd, releve Tap R BK 4th, plie	Fists next to chest, elbows BK
7-8	Grande plie (hold 4th POS) CT 7, Releve CT 8	Both circle L and shoot parallel OVRHD
1 8	RPT above	

JAZZ WALK—TRIPLES

FT 1st PP   Lock arms

A forward progression of three steps done in 2 counts of music.

COUNTS	BODY MOVEMENT	ARM MOVEMENT
1	**Step R FWD "plie-releve" POS**	**DWN**
&2	**Step L-R (plie-releve), 4th POS**	**ISOL L SHL CT 2, LJA**
3&4	**REV L-R-L, travel FWD**	**ISOL R SHL CT 4, LJA**
5-8	**RPT above traveling BK**	

TRIPLE SQUARE

(Triples FWD, BK, R, L)

1&2	**Triplet R-L-R FWD ("plie-releve" POS)**	**LJA 2nd, ISOL opp SHL**
3&4	**Triplet L-R-L BK**	
5&6	**Triplet R-L-R S8**	
7&8	**Triplet L-R-L S6**	

Triples also done moving across floor with arms crossing front of chest and diagonal opposition to forward foot.

Triples are also done OPEN and CROSSED.

OPEN position triples are done with pelvis facing direction traveling.

CROSSED position triples are done with torso twist (pelvis faces S6, shoulders front). Crossed position triples are used with same port de bras as the triple square and may be done in a square.

4th PLIE-RELEVE POSITION

CROSSED TRIPLE FORWARD

"Protein builds muscles. A body must have enough protein, or muscles will not become stronger, no matter how hard you work."

JAZZ WALK TRIPLE SQUARE WITH PORT DE BRAS

FT 1st PP   Lock arms 1st

COUNTS	BODY MOVEMENT	ARM MOVEMENT

LONG JAZZ ARM

1-8	Jazz Triple (R,L,R) Square (FWD, BK, R side, L side)	Lift both 2nd POS LJA on 1 Press both DWN on &2 RPT 3-8

LONG JAZZ ARM

JAZZ HAND SWING

1-8	Jazz Triple Square	Cross fists at waist on 1 Swing up and open 2nd POS JH on &2. RPT 3-8

CROSS AT WAIST

LOCOMOTIVE

1-8	Jazz Triple Square	Arms bent at elbow, fists, held close at waist. Circular motion (circle FWD, DWN, up) RPT 3-8

ELBOWS PULL BACK

FT 1st PP   HNDS on pelvis

COUNTS	BODY MOVEMENT	ARM MOVEMENT

JAZZ WRIST PRESS

1&2	Triple FWD R-L-R	Circle BK of R HND to R SHL on 1; press to 2nd with flexed wrist on 2 — L on pelvis
3&4	Triple BK L-R-L	REV L
5-8	RPT triples R and L	RPT R and L
1-8	RPT all above	

Also done using opposite arms.
Also done isolation opposition shoulder forward.

WRIST PRESS

JAZZ WALK TRIPLES ACROSS FLOOR WITH PORT DE BRAS
FT 1st PP   Arms 1st

Triples across the floor are done with arms in opposition 4th position. In the following techniques the triples remain the same. The Jazz Port de Bras and torso change and accents change.

VARIATION #1—4th OPPOSITION
  Arms 4th POS on CT 2. Change on CT 3.

VARIATION #2—ACCENT PRESS DWN ON 2
  Arms 4th POS on 1. Press DWN at sides on "& 2."

VARIATION #3—ACCENT UP ON 2
  Arms cross FRT of body on 1. Open 2nd POS on 2.
  ISOL SHL in opposition to FWD FT, CT 2.

VARIATION #4—TORSO SPIRAL
  Torso spirals R on R triple (like side stretch R). Arms V POS OVRHD (circle R, BK, L and end on R side).

4th OPPOSITION	ACCENT PRESS DOWN	ACCENT UP	TORSO SPIRAL

JAZZ TRIPLES WITH HEAD ISOLATIONS

FT 1st PP, lock   Fists on pelvis

COUNTS	BODY MOVEMENT	ARM MOVEMENT
&1	Step R FWD, plie, AST swing HD L to R	2nd POS, clenched fists
&2	Step L AST swing HD L	Same
3&4	Jazz triple R AST HD circles R, HD accents R	
5-8	REV	
1-8	RPT—add OPP SHL ISOL at end of triple	
1-8	RPT—traveling BK	
1-16	RPT—traveling R and L	
1-16	RPT—taking 3 step turn on triple	

HEAD SWING RIGHT

JAZZ WALK TRIPLES WITH SHOULDER ISOLATIONS

FT 1st PP, lock   Arms 1st

COUNTS	BODY MOVEMENT	ARM MOVEMENT
1-2	Walk R-L, NTO, plie	Opposition, reaching FWD
3&4	Jazz triple R, ISOL L SHL FWD on 4 (Step R, L, R)	2nd POS LJA on 3 2nd POS JH on 4
5-8	REV L	
1-8	RPT using "plie-releve" POS	Same
1-16	RPT all above	

SHOULDER ISOLATION

JAZZ TRIPLES WITH HIP ISOLATIONS

FT 1st PP, lock   Arms 1st

COUNTS	BODY MOVEMENT	ARM MOVEMENT
1&2	Plie triple FWD R-L-R, plie, ISOL hip R on 2 — identical (R hip R FT)	2nd LJA
3&4	Triple L-R-L, ISOL hip L on 2	
5-8	RPT—travel BK	
1&2	Triple R-L-R, ISOL hip L on 2 — opposition — travel FWD	LJA 2nd
3&4	REV L	
5-8	RPT — travel BK	
1&2	Triple R-L-R FWD, CON pelvis on 2	LJA 2nd CT 1, jazz HNDS CT 2
3&4	Triple L-R-L, release pelvis on 4	
5-8	RPT — BK	
1&2	Triple R-L-R FWD, circle hip R, end R	Press R wrist 2nd on CT 2
3&4	REV L	REV
5-8	RPT — BK	

HIP ISOLATION—IDENTICAL

JAZZ TRIPLES WITH RIB-CAGE ISOLATIONS

FT 1st PP, lock   Arms 1st

COUNTS	BODY MOVEMENT	ARM MOVEMENT
1&2	Plie triple FWD R-L-R, plie, ISOL rib-cage R on 2 — identical	2nd, LJA
3&4	REV L	
5-8	RPT—travel BK	
1-8	RPT triple with opp. RC	Same
1&2	Triple R-L-R, contract rib-cage on 2	JH 2nd on 2
3&4	Triple L-R-L, release rib cage on 4	LJA 2nd, pull BK elbows on 4
5-8	RPT — BK	
1-24	RPT all above	

RIB-CAGE ISOLATION
—IDENTICAL

LINDY COMBINATIONS

COUNTS	BODY MOVEMENT	ARM MOVEMENT
1&2	Side Triple—R, L, R to R	Swing to 2nd POS LJA 1&2
3-4	Step L (X BK R), step R FWD	Cross wrists at waist 3, 4
5-8	REV	

The above is a simple Lindy R and L. Variations include FWD and BK movements and different Port de Bras.

CROSSED WRISTS—LINDY

FUNKY LINDY (Accent up on the beat)

&1&2	Triple FWD with Funky torso, R-L-R	Locomotive arms
&3	Funky hip lift, step L BK	L wrist circle at L hip
&4	Step R FWD	R wrist circle at R hip
5-8	REV above moving BK	
1-8	RPT above moving R and L	

FUNKY LOCOMOTIVE ARMS

LINDY VARIATION #1 (Developpe Kick)

FT 1st PP, lock   Arms 1st

COUNTS	BODY MOVEMENT	ARM MOVEMENT
1&2	Side triple R, L, R to R	Both swing OVRHD R to L, clenched fists
&	Step L X BK R	HNDS at chest
3	Developpe R C#1, AST CON torso — L "plie-releve" POS	Push flexed wrist C1
4	Step R C1, plie	DWN R
5-8	REV L	
1-8	RPT all R and L	

DEVELOPPE AND
TORSO CONTRACTION

SIDE WALKING TURNS

Easiest form to begin: FT 1st PP, plie   Arms 1st

COUNTS	BODY MOVEMENT	ARM MOVEMENT
1	Step R 2nd POS plie, NTO	LJA 2nd POS
2	XLOR, turning R	HNDS at chest
&3	Step R completing R turn face CT 1, PT L 2nd.	4th POS, R 2nd, L FWD
4	Hold above POS, plie (Entire turn done in plie)	Hold
5-8	REV L	
1-8	RPT above	
	Also done to S7 and S5 (upstage and DWN stage)	
	Also done with HD REL on "&4"	

HOLD AT
END OF TURN

VARIATION: Add two walks before walking turn

1-2	Walk R-L FWD	Opposition
3&4	R walking turn	Same as above
5-8	REV to L turn	

JAZZ INSIDE TURN

FT 1st PP, plie   Arms 1st

COUNTS	BODY MOVEMENT	ARM MOVEMENT
1-2	Walk FWD R-L, NTO, plie	Arms DWN
3	Neutral passe R	Chest
4	Step R 2nd POS	4th POS, R FRT
5-6	One single inside trn R, tap L 2nd (L neutral passe during turn)	Chest on 5, 2nd LJA on 6
7-8	RPT turn	Same
1-8	REV L	
1-16	RPT R and L	
	Done moving across floor	
	Done moving in a square (R side, L side, up stage and DWN stage)	

NEUTRAL PASSE

OUTSIDE PAS DE BOUREE TURN

FT 1st PP, plie   Arms 1st

COUNTS	BODY MOVEMENT	ARM MOVEMENT
1	Step R to R, releve	LJA 2nd
2	XLOR, plie	4th POS opposition (R FWD)
3&4	Step R-L-releve, turning R.	DWN 1st
	Step R FWD plie (pas de bouree)	
5-8	REV L	Same as above
1-8	RPT all above	
	Also done moving BK and FWD	
	Also done in sequence without 2 step preparation in between; and 3 pas de bouree turns (R and L and R)	

CROSS LEFT OVER RIGHT
—4th POSITION ARMS

JAZZ INSIDE TURNS ON ONE LEG

FT 1st PP, lock   Arms 1st

COUNTS	BODY MOVEMENT	ARM MOVEMENT
1	Neutral passe R, plie, NTO	2nd LJA
2	Step R FWD in plie	4th POS (R FRT)
3&	Inside turn on R leg, plie.	HNDS at chest
	HD spots FRT on "&" CT.	
4	Step L, locked knee	DWN
	RPT 3 Xs	
	REV by tapping L — no weight on 4th turn	
	Also done 2nd POS	
	Also done in multiples (two turns on CTS 3&)	
	Also done on half toe with locked supporting leg (pique)	

NEUTRAL PASSE

2 STEP TURN WITH CHASSE HIP LEAD—TORSO TWIST

FT 1st PP, locked knees   Arms 1st

COUNTS	BODY MOVEMENT	ARM MOVEMENT
1&2	Inside R turn, step R FWD, plie, turn R L at neutral passe, step L FWD CT 2, plie	4th POS (R FRT, CT 1) HNDS at chest on "&" CT
3&4	Chasse FWD R-L-R — torso twist (lead with hip), plie	4th POS, ISOL R SHL (L FWD)
5-8	REV L (travel X FLR)	
1-8	RPT all above	

TORSO TWIST

OUTSIDE TURNS

FT 1st PP, locked knees   Arms 1st

COUNTS	BODY MOVEMENT	ARM MOVEMENT
1&2	Triple R-L-R FWD, NTO, plie (4th POS preparation)	Swing up to 4th POS (L FRT)
3&	Outside turn L, plie, neutral passe L	HNDS at chest
4	Step L, plie, NTO	1st POS
5-8	Done moving across room	
	Also can be used for multiple turns (2 turns, CTS 3&)	
1-8	REV for R turns	

PREPARATION FOR
OUTSIDE TURN

COMBINATION TURNS

FT 1st PP, plie   Arms 2nd LJA

COUNTS	BODY MOVEMENT	ARM MOVEMENT
1-2-3	Step R-L-releve (pas de bouree turn R) Step R FWD plie	Reach OVRHD & DWN on CT 2
4	Hold 4th POS R FWD	4th POS (L FWD, R 2nd)
5-6	OTL (single)	Chest
7-8	Step FWD L-R demi-plie, NTO	Arms in opposition
1-8	REV L	
1-16	RPT R and L	Same as above
	Also done with multiple turns (2 turns CTS 5&6)	

END OF
PAS BOUREE TURN

OUTSIDE TURN PROMENADE WITH ARABESQUE & ATTITUDE PIVOT
Done in progressions quarter, half, full
FT 1st PP, locked knees   Arms 1st

COUNTS	BODY MOVEMENT	ARM MOVEMENT
	QUARTER TURNS	
1-2	Step R-L FWD, plie, NTO	Opposition
3-4	Arabesque R low AST pivot on L leg to side 8 (¼ turn R) — Lift heel to pivot.	4th POS (R FRT, L 2nd)
5-6	Pivot S#7	
7-8	Pivot S#6	
	Spot HD in each direction	
1-8	RPT	
1-16	REV by starting L	
	HALF TURN PIVOT — FULL TURN PIVOT	
1-2	Step R-L FWD	
3-4	Pivot S#7 with R arabesque (½ turn)	
5-6	Pivot S#5 (½ turn)	
7-8	Full turn to face S#5	
1-8	RPT	
1-16	REV by starting L	
	Also done with BK leg in attitude	

ARABESQUE PIVOT

KNEE TURNS
FT 1st PP, locked knees   Arms 1st

COUNTS	BODY MOVEMENT	ARM MOVEMENT
1-2	Step R-L (FWD to grande-plie)	L FWD CT 1, 4th POS, R FWD CT 2
3&4	R knee, L knee, 1 full turn R (on knees — lift FT, step R CT 4)	Chest
5-6	Stand and step L-R FWD	R FWD CT 5 4th POS, L FWD, CT 6
7&8	Turn L knee, R knee, step L	Chest
1-8	RPT R and L	

PREPARATION FOR
KNEE TURN

Jazz Adage

JAZZ ADAGE I

Adage is done slowly and technically clean, taking full amount of counts to complete each slow 8 count phrase. Slow adage builds technique and control.

COUNTS	BODY MOVEMENT	ARM MOVEMENT
1-4	Turn R knee in 2nd POS, plie	R circles 2nd and OVRHD

KNEE TURNED-IN
SECOND

5-8	Lunge R to 2nd (R side)	R reaches 2nd on 5,6 L reaches 2nd on 7,8
1-4	Lunge R FWD, 4th POS	Both circle OVRHD into chest and to 2nd POS LJA
5-8	Continue, deeper R lunge FWD	ISOL L SHL FWD 5,6 ISOL R SHL FWD 7,8
1-4	Single OTL (done slowly and technically correct)	Into chest
5-8	High hip lift L, step L on CT 8	4th POS, R FWD, L 2nd

HIGH HIP LIFT

1-2	Brush R attitude to C#2	2nd POS, LJA
3-4	Brush R attitude to C#1	Same
5-6	Ronde de jambe R (keep leg at waist height)	Same
7-8	R BK attitude, still face C#1	Same
1-4	Turn in R knee and lunge BK to C#4	R arm circle 2nd and OVRHD
5-8	Continue, deeper R lunge to C#4	R reaches 2nd to C#4 L reaches 2nd to C#2
1-2	Torso FRT	Swing to 4th POS; R FRT, L 2nd
3-4	Single OTR, plie	Into chest
5-8	Lunge FWD R	2nd LJA, ISOL L SHL FWD 5,6 ISOL R SHL FWD 7,8

LUNGE FORWARD

1-8	R slides FWD into split (face FRT) (full split or jazz split)	2nd LJA
1-4	Swastika POS (R FRT, L BK)	Same
5-6	Lift to both knees (kneeling)	Same
7-8	Step L, R FWD (standing POS)	1st POS
8-8's	REV all to L (turn in L)	

BATTEMENT SERIES

4th POS, R PT BK, locked knees   Arms 1st

COUNTS	BODY MOVEMENT	ARM MOVEMENT
&1	Step R-L (BK-FRT), plie, NTO	2nd POS LJA
2	Battement R FWD, PT toe, releve L	
3&4	Triple FWD R-L-R, NTO, plie	Cross FRT of chest and 2nd LJA
5-8	REV L	
&1	Step R-L (4th BK-FRT), plie	2nd POS LJA
2	Battement R 2nd POS, PT toe	Same
3&4	Side triple S#8, R-L-R	V OVRHD and jazz HNDS 2nd
5-8	REV L	
&1	Step R-L (4th BK-FRT)	2nd LJA
2	Battement R BK (arabesque)	4th (R FRT)
3&4	Triple R-L-R (BK, BK, FRT)	
5-8	REV L	
3-8's	RPT all above	SECOND BATTEMENT

Variations on the Battement Series would include different port de bras and variations on the battement leg and the supporting leg.

Examples would be:
1. flexed foot battement
2. flexed supporting leg with releve
3. releve supporting leg with locked knee

An intermediate variation could add an arch or back or side lay-out to the torso following the battement.

Example:

COUNTS	BODY MOVEMENT	ARM MOVEMENT
&1	Step R-L (BK-FRT), plie	Cross wrists
2	Battement R FWD, L "plie-releve" POS	2nd POS LJA or JH
3	Release BK, "plie-releve" POS on L knee	2nd or R BK, L FRT folded at waist
4	Step R FWD, plie, NTO	
5-8	REV	FORWARD BATTEMENT,
1-8	RPT all above	"PLIE-RELEVE" POSITION

JAZZ ADAGE II

COUNTS	BODY MOVEMENT	ARM MOVEMENT
1-4	Ronde de jambe R to C#4 (turn L, end in 4th POS, L in deep lunge)	2nd POS LJA, and press to 4th POS on CTS 3, 4. R FWD, L 2nd
5-8	Grande-plie 2nd, turn R face C#2, lock knees on 7, 8	Jazz HNDS 2nd POS
1-8	Hold 4 POS, facing C#2 Plie 1,2 — releve 3,4 "Plie-releve" POS 5,8	1,2 chest — 3,4 OVRHD 5,8 DIAG press (L FWD, R BK)

4th "PLIE-RELEVE" POSITION

1-4	Ronde de jambe L to C#3 (turn R end in 4th POS, R in deep lunge	2nd POS LJA, and press to 4th POS on CTS 3,4 — L FWD, R 2nd
5-8	Grande-plie 2nd, turn L face C#1, lock knees on 7,8	Jazz HNDS 2nd POS
1-8	RPT "plie-releve" port de bras as above	Chest, OVRHD, DIAG
1-4	Lunge R to C#1, TBTP BK	V POS OVRHD
5-8	Torso twist to C#4 (hold lunge)	Same
1-4	Lunge L to C#2, TBTP BK	V POS OVRHD
5-8	Torso twist to C#3 (hold lunge)	Same
1-4	XROL corkscrew turn L (start releve end plie 4th POS on FLR)	LJA 2nd

CORKSCREW TURN

5-6	Slow ascend	LJA 2nd, accent elbows lifting
7-8	Demi-plie 4th POS, L BK — HD pulls BK	Circle HNDS into SHLS and press palms FWD
1-8	REV above—XLOR corkscrew turn R, etc.	Same
1-2	Step R FT BK, plie	Jazz HNDS 2nd POS
3-4	Passe L turned out, lock R knee	High 4th (R OVRHD)
5-6	Plie R CT 5, lock R 6, develope L	2nd LJA
7-8	Step L FWD, R BK	1st POS
1-8	REV above (step BK L plie)	Same as above
1-16	RPT above combination stepping R to 2nd, develope L 2nd (CTS 7, 8 step L BK, FRT) Also RPT to L.	Same
12-8's	RPT entire adage from beginning (ronde de jambe R)	

JAZZ ADAGE III—Contraction and Sous-Sus

FT 4th POS, L BK   Arms 2nd LJA   ISOL L SHL FWD

COUNTS	BODY MOVEMENT	ARM MOVEMENT
1-4	Step R 2nd, TI R knee, CON pelvis and RC, face C #2	2nd jazz HNDS

PELVIS AND
RC CONTRACTION

5-8	Sous-Sus (R FRT 5th), lock balance and hold	2nd LJA
1-4	Hold Sous-Sus, demi-plie (slowly)	2nd jazz HNDS
5-8	Lock knees (slowly)	Same
1-4	Demi-plie 5th, CTS 1, 2—lock 3, 4 ISOL L SHL FWD on 1, 2—RET 3, 4	R circles OVRHD and 2nd jazz HND, L HND at pelvis, both arms 1st CTS 3, 4

ISOLATION LEFT SHOULDER

5-8	REV above 4 CTS with L SHL ISOL	REV arms (L arm circles)
1-4	Grande plie 5th POS	V POS OVRHD

GRANDE PLIE 5th

5-8	Lift to standing POS, heels on FLR, knees lock	Thru 2nd to 1st
4-8's	REV and RPT all above L (Step L 2nd TI knee)	RPT above
8,8's	RPT all above R and L	Same

JAZZ ADAGE III—Contraction and Sous-Sus

FT 4th POS, L BK   Arms 2nd LJA   ISOL L SHL FWD

COUNTS	BODY MOVEMENT	ARM MOVEMENT
1-4	Step R 2nd, TI R knee, CON pelvis and RC, face C #2	2nd jazz HNDS

PELVIS AND
RC CONTRACTION

5-8	Sous-Sus (R FRT 5th), lock balance and hold	2nd LJA
1-4	Hold Sous-Sus, demi-plie (slowly)	2nd jazz HNDS
5-8	Lock knees (slowly)	Same
1-4	Demi-plie 5th, CTS 1, 2—lock 3, 4 ISOL L SHL FWD on 1, 2—RET 3, 4	R circles OVRHD and 2nd jazz HND, L HND at pelvis, both arms 1st CTS 3, 4

ISOLATION LEFT SHOULDER

5-8	REV above 4 CTS with L SHL ISOL	REV arms (L arm circles)
1-4	Grande plie 5th POS	V POS OVRHD

GRANDE PLIE 5th

5-8	Lift to standing POS, heels on FLR, knees lock	Thru 2nd to 1st
4-8's	REV and RPT all above L (Step L 2nd TI knee)	RPT above
8,8's	RPT all above R and L	Same

Sample Combination

SAMPLE COMBINATION #1

FT 2nd PP, lock   Fists on pelvis

COUNTS	BODY MOVEMENT	ARM MOVEMENT

STEP 1

1-2	Step R-L FWD, NTO, demi-plie	2nd, LJA
3	DEV kick R FWD, L "plie-releve"	Same

DEVELOPE KICK FORWARD

4-5-6	P.D.B. turn R and 4th POS, R FRT (Step R, L, R)	DWN for turn end, 4th POS for preparation (L arm FWD, R 2nd)
7-8	OTL—plie	Into chest
1-8	REV	
1-16	RPT	

STEP 2

1-2	Step R-L FWD, NTO, demi-plie	DWN
3&4	Triple R-L-R (torso twist), pelvis L side	4th POS (L FWD, R 2nd)

TORSO TWIST

5-6	Walk BK L-R	DWN
7&8	Triple BK L-R-L twist, pelvis R	
1-8	Also done traveling S-R and S-L	Same

Jazz Wrist Press ISOL

1-2	Step R-L FWD	DWN
3&4	Triple R-L-R	R jazz wrist press 2nd

WRIST PRESS SECOND

5-6	Walk FWD L-R	DWN
7&8	Triple L-R-L	L jazz wrist press 2nd
1-8	RPT (travel BK)	Same

STEP 3

HEAD ISOLATION

1-2	Step R-L FWD, swing HD R, L	Fists on pelvis

HEAD SWING RIGHT

3&4	Triple R-L-R FWD AST ISOL HD 1 full circle R and accent R on CT 4	2nd POS, LJA
5-6	Step FWD L-R, swing HD, L, R	DWN
7&8	Triple BK L-R-L AST ISOL HD (full circle accent L on CT 8)	2nd, LJA
1-8	RPT above	Same

SAMPLE COMBINATION #2

COUNTS	BODY MOVEMENT	ARM MOVEMENT
1-2	Step R-L FWD 4th POS NTO, demi-plie	L wrist FWD 2, R 2nd
3&4	Rotate pelvis (Fig. 8 L to R)	

PELVIS ROTATION

5&6	Travel DIAG C1, L-R-L, no WT L (PT L 2nd POS)	
7	XLOR	R OVRHD, L 2nd
8	Tap R 2nd	R arm 2nd
1-2	OTR, step R FWD CT 2	Fists OVRHD
3-4	Walk BK L-R	
&5	Sous-Sus L-R to L (L BK)	2nd
6	Step L FWD	
7	XROL	Both reach OVRHD V POS
&8	High hip lift L and step L	2nd LJA
1-16	RPT 16 CTS above	Same

XROL—ARMS
V POSITION OVERHEAD

Comparison of Modern Jazz and Rock Jazz Techniques

MODERN JAZZ and ROCK JAZZ
Comparison Technique of Both Forms of Jazz

Since Jazz Dance is dominated by Jazz Music, there are different styles of Modern Jazz movement and they seem to fall into the following categories:

> Afro-Primitive Jazz
> Lyric Jazz
> Modern Jazz
> Musical Comedy Jazz
> Rock Jazz

Rock Jazz is the most popular because of the popularity of rock music.

MODERN JAZZ	ROCK JAZZ
Accent is down on 1 Count.	Accent is up on 1 count (plie on "and" count before the 1 count).
Isolations are opposite to feet.	Isolations are identical to feet.
Movements are sharp and accented.	Movements are freer and not as exaggerated.
Head moves in sharp, clean directions.	Head moves in swinging and circular rhythm.
Pelvis moves in sharp direction focus.	Pelvis moves easily with a back motion (released)

In the following analysis, the movements of Modern Jazz and Rock Jazz are compared, using the same combinations and adapting them to each style. Remember: Modern Jazz usually maintains the demi-plie position, and Rock accents the up position with demi-plie preceding the beat.

COUNTS	BODY MOVEMENT	ARM MOVEMENT

BOUNCE PULSE

Modern Jazz Style

1-8	Stand FT together 1st POS NTO Bend knees on even CTS; STR on odd CTS	1st POS

Rock Style

&1-8	Same as above except bend knees on "&" CTS, STR on CT. (Note: Always plie on "&" CT preceding the beat.)	1st POS

COUNTS	BODY MOVEMENT	ARM MOVEMENT

BOUNCE WALK

Modern Jazz Style

1	Step FWD R	1st POS
2	Bounce with L in neutral passe	
3-4	REV (accent DWN 2, 4, 6, 8)	
5-8	RPT above R and L	

Rock Style

&1	Plie L, lift R and step R on CT 1	1st POS
&2	Plie R and step L	
3-4	REV (accent up 2, 4, 6, 8)	
5-8	RPT above R and L	

HIP WALK

Modern Jazz Style—ISOL OPP

1-2	Step FWD R, isolating L hip to L side—tap L next to R on CT 2	L jazz HND FWD, R BK
3-4	REV	
5-8	RPT above	

MODERN JAZZ HIP WALK,
ISOLATIONS OPPOSITE TO
FORWARD FOOT

Rock Style—ISOL IDENTICAL

&1&2	ISOL R hip and Tap R and Step R on CT 2	Circle R FWD and wrist press
&3&4	Same to L	L on pelvis
5-8	RPT	

ROCK JAZZ HIP WALK,
ISOLATIONS IDENTICAL TO
FORWARD FOOT

"The best dancers are total dancers; they study all forms of movement: ballet, modern dance, tap and jazz."

COUNTS	BODY MOVEMENT	ARM MOVEMENT

SIDE JAZZ WALK

Modern Jazz Style

1	Step R to 2nd, ISOL L hip	2nd POS on CT 1
2	Tap—close L to R, hip BK to neutral	Cross arms FRT on CT 2
3-8	RPT L, R, L	

Rock Style

&1	Hip lift R and step R	Pull R BK from elbow
&2	Tap—close L to R	
3-4	REV	
5-8	RPT above	

PELVIS SQUARE

Modern Jazz Style

1-2	Step R FWD and CON pelvis	Both arms FWD FRT of SHL
3-4	Step L FWD, ISOL R hip to side	2nd POS
5-6	Step R, ISOL L hip to side	2nd POS
7-8	Step L and CON pelvis	FWD FRT of SHL

Rock Style

&1&2	Step R FWD and REL pelvis	Pull both arms BK from elbow
&3&4	Step L FWD, ISOL L hip to side	Pull L BK from elbow
&5&6	Step R, ISOL R hip	Pull R BK from elbow
&7&8	Step L, REL pelvis	Pull both BK from elbow

PELVIS AND RIB-CAGE MOVEMENT

Modern Jazz Style

&1	CON and step R to side	Both arms FWD FRT of SHL
2	Tap—Close L to R, hip to neutral	1st POS
3-4	REV	
5-8	RPT above (also done on beat)	

Rock Style (Funky Movement)

&1	REL and step R on locked knee to side	Pull both arms BK from elbow
&2	Tap—close L on plie	
&3,4	REV	
5-8	RPT above (also done on beat)	

COUNTS	BODY MOVEMENT	ARM MOVEMENT

TRIPLE PELVIS

Modern Jazz Style

1&2	ISOL hips L, R, L and step R on CT 2	2nd POS
3&4	ISOL hips R, L, R and step L on CT 4	
5-8	RPT above	

Rock Style

&1&2	ISOL hips R, L, R and step R on CT 2	Fists lift to SHL R, L, R
3&4	REV	REV
5-8	RPT above	

HEAD MOVEMENT

(May be adapted to either style depending on choreography.) The following exercises done with FT together 1st POS NTO.

Single "Yes" Movement

1-8	Head up on odd CTS and DWN on even CTS

Double "Yes" Movement

&1-&8	HD up on "&" CTS, DWN on the beats

Single "No" Movement

1-8	HD turns to R on odd CTS, L on even CTS

Double "No" Movement

&1-&8	HD turns R on "&" CTS, L on the beats

Head Swing

1-2	HD DWN on CT 1, to R on CT 2
3-4	REV
5-8	RPT above (also done on beat)

Head Thrust

1-2	Push HD FWD on CT 1, BK to CTR on CT 2
3-8	RPT 3 Xs

Double Head Thrust

&1-&8	Push FWD on "&" CTS, CTR on beats

Head Tilt

1-8	Keeping face parallel to FRT, HD is CTR on odd CTS, tilted to R on even CTS
1-8	REV to L

Double Head Tilt

&1-&8	HD is CTR on "&" CTS, to side on beats (8 CTS R and 8 CTS L)

COUNTS	BODY MOVEMENT	ARM MOVEMENT

SHOULDER MOVEMENTS

Shoulder Rotation—Modern Jazz Style

COUNTS	BODY MOVEMENT	ARM MOVEMENT
1-2	Step R FWD, rotate L SHL **FWD**	2nd POS jazz HND
3-4	REV	
5-8	RPT above	

Shoulder Rotation—Rock Style

COUNTS	BODY MOVEMENT	ARM MOVEMENT
&1,2	Step R, rotate R SHL **BK**—REL pelvis	Pull R BK from elbow
&3,4	REV	REV
5-8	RPT above	

ARM MOVEMENTS

Arm Swing—Modern Jazz Style

COUNTS	BODY MOVEMENT	ARM MOVEMENT
1-2	Walk FWD R	L arm swings FRT from SHL, R swings 2nd from elbow
3-4	FWD L	R swings FRT from elbow and L to 2nd from SHL
5-8	RPT above	

Arm Swing—Rock Style

COUNTS	BODY MOVEMENT	ARM MOVEMENT
1-8	Same as Modern Jazz except both arms swing R and L from **ELBOW**	

Locomotive Arms—Modern Jazz Style

COUNTS	BODY MOVEMENT	ARM MOVEMENT
1-8	Walk FWD, 2 CTS for each step (R,L,R,L) (Also done on beat)	Arms bent at elbow and held in close to waist. Circle L FWD, then R (as "choo choo" train motion)

Locomotive Arms—Rock Style

COUNTS	BODY MOVEMENT	ARM MOVEMENT
&1-8	Same as above except both arms move FWD and BK AST (Also done on beat)	

COUNTS	BODY MOVEMENT	ARM MOVEMENT

FLAT FOOT WALK

Modern Jazz Style

COUNTS	BODY MOVEMENT	ARM MOVEMENT
1-2	Step R, plie	Swing arms in opposition
3-4	REV	to FWD FT
5-8	RPT	

Rock Style

COUNTS	BODY MOVEMENT	ARM MOVEMENT
&1,2	Step R in plie, STR—REL pelvis	Circle R in from elbow and push FWD with heel of HND
3-4	REV	
5-8	RPT	

BODY MOVEMENT

Step R, Tap Left—Modern Jazz Style

COUNTS	BODY MOVEMENT	ARM MOVEMENT
1&2	Step R to side, plie R on "&" CT, tap L FWD	Swing R arm FWD FRT of SHL
3&4	REV	REV
5-8	RPT all above	Use both arms (R FWD, L BK)

Step Right, Tap Left—Rock Style

COUNTS	BODY MOVEMENT	ARM MOVEMENT
&1&2	Step R to side, plie R on "&" CT, tap L FWD	Circle and push L wrist FWD on CT 2
3&4	REV	
5-8	RPT all above	Use both arms (R FWD, L BK)

"Moving should be a habit—like eating or sleeping."

Hops, Jumps, Leaps

HOPS, JUMPS, LEAPS
(In ballet they are called Saute)

JUMP—Taking off and landing on both feet

LEAP—Taking off with one foot and landing on the other foot.
Also taking off from both feet and landing on one foot.

HOP—Taking off and landing on the same foot

SAUTE—Any movement leaving the floor

As in any form of dance, all jumps, leaps or hops must start in demi-plie and finish in demi-plie. Jumps are done at end of class. Jumps should be practiced in 1st and 2nd positions turned out. Small jumps are practiced first with stress placed on plie, locked knees and pointed toes. After this has been accomplished, dancer strives for elevation. Ballet theory for jumps should be followed.

1st POSITION JUMPS NTO (Quarter Turn Right)

FT 1st PP, lock   Fists at pelvis

COUNTS	BODY MOVEMENT	ARM MOVEMENT
1-4	Walk FWD plie R-L-R-L 3#5 (FT together CT 4)	DWN 1st POS
&5	Plie and Jump 1st POS NTO, face S#5	

FIRST POSITION JUMP

&6	RPT face S#8	
&7	RPT face S#7	
&8	RPT face S#6	
	Also done with a head tilt (and side stretch), R-L-R-L	Jazz HNDS 1st

JUMP AND HEAD TILT
AND SIDE STRETCH

Add claps to the 4 walks
Progress to ½ and full turns — see next page

1st POSITION JUMPS NTO (Two half turns and one full turn)

1-4	Walk FWD R-L-R-L (FT together CT 4)	Clap on each step
&5&6	Jump R to face S#7, jump R to face S#5	
&7-8	1 full turn R end facing S#5	Into chest
1-8	REV L	1st POS

PRANCE

FT 1st POS NTO, locked knees   Arms 1st

COUNTS	BODY MOVEMENT	ARM MOVEMENT
&1	Hop to R, L low attitude FRT, TO, plie	2nd POS, LJA
&2	REV L (traveling FWD)	Same

PRANCE

&3-8	RPT
1-8	RPT all above

PRANCE WITH SHOULDER ISOLATION

&1	Hop to R, L low attitude FRT AST ISOL R SHL	2nd POS, LJA

PRANCE—SHOULDER ISOLATION

&2-8	REV and RPT
1-8	RPT all above

JUMP WITH STOMP

FT 1st POS, NTO, locked knees   Arms 1st

COUNTS	BODY MOVEMENT	ARM MOVEMENT
&1	Jump 1st POS in place NTO	OVRHD
2	Stomp R FWD NTO and no weight	Push HNDS FWD of chest
&3-6	REV L, RPT R	
7-8	Walk BK R, L, plie	DWN
&1-8	RPT all above	

JUMP WITH
STOMP FORWARD

JUMP-STOMP QUARTER TURNS

&1-2	Turning R, jump-stomp R (face S#8)	Same as preceding page
&3-4	Turning R, REV jump-stomp L (face S#7)	
&5-6	Jump-stomp R (face S#6)	
7-8	(Face FRT) Walk BK R-L, plie	
1-8	REV beginning L and turning L	

HALF TURNS

&1-2	Jump-stomp R facing FRT	Same as above
&3-4	Jump-stomp L turning R (face S#7)	
5-6	Turning R, jump-stomp R (face S#5)	
7-8	Walk BK R, L, plie	
1-8	REV to L side	

FULL TURNS ARE TAUGHT IN INTERMEDIATE LEVEL

PASSE JUMPS

FT 1st POS, NTO, locked knees   Arms 1st

COUNTS	BODY MOVEMENT	ARM MOVEMENT
1-2	Run FWD R-L, plie, NTO	2nd
&	Plie R FWD	Cross FRT of chest
3	Hop R, passe L, NTO (lock R knee in air, PT toes)	High 4th (R up, L 2nd)
4	Land R	4th high
5-8	REV L	
1-8	RPT all above	
	Done moving across FLR or FWD and BK	

HOP—PASSE

BATTEMENT 2ND WITH SAUTE HOP

FT 1st POS, NTO, locked knees   Arms 1st

COUNTS	BODY MOVEMENT	ARM MOVEMENT
1-2	Run R-L FWD	LJA 2nd
3	XROL, plie	Cross FRT
&4	Battement L 2nd POS AST saute—hop R	2nd POS, ILJA
5-8	REV	
1-8	RPT all above	
	Also done moving BK, or In big circle R	

SAUTE—
BATTEMENT SECOND

JETE WITH TRIPLE

FT 1st POS, NTO, locked knees   Arms 1st

COUNTS	BODY MOVEMENT	ARM MOVEMENT
1&2	Triple step R-L-R FWD, plie	LJA 2nd
3	Step L FWD, plie	1st POS
&4	Jete R FWD, plie	4th POS (L FWD, R 2nd)
5-8	REV L	
1-8	RPT all above	
	Also done traveling the DIAG C1 and C2	
	Also done in big circle	

JETE

STAG LEAP—UPRIGHT POSITION

FT 1st POS, NTO, locked knees   Arms 1st

COUNTS	BODY MOVEMENT	ARM MOVEMENT
1-2	Step R-L FWD	2nd
3	Plie 5th POS prep for leap (R FRT)	DWN
&4	Leap R FWD L attitude BK, NTO (R FT to L knee—stag)	High 4th (L FWD, R 2nd)
5-8	REV L	
1-8	RPT all above	Same

UPRIGHT STAG LEAP

BATTEMENT—JETE COMBINATION

FT 1st POS, NTO, locked knees   Arms 1st

COUNTS	BODY MOVEMENT	ARM MOVEMENT
1	XROL—plie	Cross FRT
&2	Battement L 2nd, Saute R	2nd, ILJA
3	XLOR—plie	Cross FRT
&4	Jete R (thrust FWD)	4th (L FRT, R 2nd)
5-8	REV	
1-8	RPT all above	

CROSS RIGHT OVER
LEFT—PLIE

JETE-ARABESQUE

4th POS, R FT BK, plie, TO   Arms 4th—R FRT, L 2nd

COUNTS	BODY MOVEMENT	ARM MOVEMENT
1	Step R FWD—plie	1st POS
&2	Jete L FWD	4th (R FRT, L 2nd)
3	Step R plie	Cross FRT of chest
&4	Arabesque L, Saute R	V POS FRT
5-8	REV	
1-8	RPT all above	

ARABESQUE—SAUTE

"Dancers are the finest-tuned athletes in the world."

Grade 3

Intermediate-Advanced Jazz Class

PRE-STRETCH WARM-UP

Done centre before floor technique—
for loosening of the body before floor stretches.
Begin 2nd POS NTO, lock   Arms DWN

COUNTS	BODY MOVEMENT	ARMS

Head Isolations

1 (Slow)	REL HD BK	DWN—first POS

RELEASE HEAD BACK

2	CON HD FWD	Same throughout
3	Tilt HD R	
4	Tilt HD L	
5-8	RPT	
1-24	RPT 3 Xs	
1-2	Swing HD L to R	
3-4	REV R to L	
5-16	RPT	
1-4	Complete Circle R	
5-8	Complete Circle L	
1-8	RPT	

Shoulder Isolations

1	Both SHL FWD	DWN—first POS same throughout
2	Both SHL UP	
3	Both SHL BK	
4	Both SHL DWN	
5-16	RPT	
1-16	REV BK-UP-FWD-DWN	
1-2	Lift R SHL, drop R SHL	

ISOLATION RIGHT
SHOULDER FORWARD

3-4	REV L
4-16	RPT
1-2	ISOL R SHL FWD and return
3-4	REV L and return
5-16	RPT

"Wear wool to keep the muscles warm and to prevent injuries."

Rib-Cage Isolations

1-2	ISOL RC R	R 2nd LJA, L on pelvis

ISOLATION—RIB-CAGE RIGHT

3-4	REV L	L 2nd LJA
5-6-7	ISOL RC R-L-R	LJA 2nd
&8	Neutral RC	DWN
1-8	REV L	
1-16	RPT all above	
1-2	CON RC	DWN, flex wrists FWD

FLEX WRISTS FORWARD—
CONTRACT RIB-CAGE

3-4	REL RC	DWN, flex wrists BK
5-6-7	CON-REL-CON	Flex wrists on CT (FWD, BK, FWD)
8	Neutral RC	DWN—press fingers to 1st
1-8	REV-REL RC	Flex wrists BK and FWD
1-16	RPT all above	

Pelvis Isolations

1-2	CON PELVIS FWD, plie, NTO, 2nd POS	Pull elbows BK (fists up)

CONTRACT PELVIS—
PULL ELBOWS BACK

3-4	REL pelvis BK, plie, NTO	Push fists FWD (fists DWN)
5-8	RPT	
1-8	RPT to corners (C#1 CT 1—neutral CT 2)	R LJA CT 1—pull elbows BK CT 2, fists up
1-4	R hip circle (circle R and return to neutral)	2nd Jazz HNDS
5-8	REV L	
1-8	RPT	
1-8	CON & REL pelvis on CT with knees locked, 2nd POS	V POS OVRHD

Knee Isolations

1	Flex R knee TO (heel off FLR)	2nd LJA

TURN-IN RIGHT KNEE

COUNTS	BODY MOVEMENT	ARMS
2	Turn R neutral	
3-4	Press R heel DWN	1st
5	Flex R knee in	2nd jazz HNDS
6	Turn R knee out	Same
7	Pulse knee outward R	4th, L DIAG FWD, R 2nd
8	R heel DWN	DWN—1st POS
1-8	REV L	
1-16	RPT R and L above	

Tabletop Torso
FT 2nd POS, NTO, locked knees
V POS OVRHD

1-4	TBTP lay-out FWD (bend from hips, face to FLR)	V POS OVRHD

TABLETOP LAY-OUT FORWARD

5-8	Drop torso TWD FLR, hang HD (pulse)	HNDS ankles

DROP TORSO

1-4	Plie and lock both knees (HD to knees)	Hold ankles
5-8	RPT	
1-4	Pull HD between legs	Hold ankles
5-8	CON upright	V POS OVRHD
1-4	TBTP BK lay-out (face to ceiling)	Wrists out, press OVRHD

LAY-OUT BACK AND
WRISTS PRESS

5-8	Recover upright POS	V POS OVRHD
1-96	RPT 3 Xs	

"When you sleep the body temperature drops and the body becomes cooler and the tendons, ligaments and muscles become stiffer—consequently, start morning stretches slowly."

▌ *Floor Stretches*

Note: See grade 1 for primary stretches used for all grades

Premise for building strength, technique and endurance. After the primary floor stretches have been mastered, the student is ready for progressions in floor work, choreographically moving from one stretch to another stretch, keeping a lyrical flow throughout the progression.

The following are progressive floor stretches for the intermediate and advanced student.

LUNGE AND PELVIS CONTRACTION
—Floor Progression

Kneeling, 1st POS   Torso upright   Arms 1st POS

COUNTS	BODY MOVEMENT	ARMS
1-2	Lunge R FT FWD NTO (keep L knee in place)	2nd POS LJA

FORWARD LUNGE RIGHT

3-4	Return R knee to 1st	1st
5-6	Lunge R 2nd TO	2nd POS LJA
7-8	Return R knee to 1st	1st
1-8	RPT and REV above lunge L FWD	Same
1-2	Lunge R FWD NTO	2nd POS LJA
3-4	Return R knee to 1st	1st
5-6	Lunge R 2nd TO	2nd POS LJA
7-8	CON pelvis only	2nd POS jazz HNDS
1-4	Sit to FLR with contracted pelvis	Same
5-8	Sit on FLR—hold (weight on R FT, bent knee—L leg on FLR, BK)	2nd POS LJA

SIT TO FLOOR FROM
2nd LUNGE

1-4	CON pelvis, lift to L knee	2nd POS jazz HNDS
5-8	Pulse to R side lunge and return R knee to 1st on FLR, on CT 8	2nd LJA, 1st on CT 8
3,8's	RPT and REV above lunge L FWD	Same

(Variation—Contraction with Locked Knee)

1-4	Lunge R FWD, lock L knee	2nd POS LJA
5-8	Turn torso L, extend L leg 2nd, flex ankle	2nd POS LJA
1-4	Contract pelvis and sit to FLR	Jazz HND 2nd POS

SIT TO FLOOR WITH
KNEE LOCKED

5-8	Hold sit	2nd LJA
1-4	CON and lift to upright POS (L leg remains extended)	Jazz HND 2nd POS
5-8	Turn torso FRT into deep lunge R	2nd POS LJA
1-4	Place L knee on FLR	Same
5-8	R knee returns to 1st	1st
4,8's	RPT and REV above lunge L	Same

*"At dance classes, regular attendance is a must—
if any results are going to be seen."*

CHOREOGRAPHED FLOOR PROGRESSION

Lyrical movement, stretching all movement to end of each phrase, dissolve to next movement. Start in fetal position, kneel on knees, head on floor at knees, hands back next to feet. Maintain slow count throughout progression. Music—4/4, lyrical rhythm—slow.

COUNTS	BODY MOVEMENT	ARMS
1-16 (Slow)	**Hold in fetal POS (on knees)**	**At sides**
1-8	**CON and lift torso to upright kneeling POS**	**Move to V POS OVRHD**
1-8	**Sit to R side (end swastika POS, R leg FRT, L BK)**	**Circle DWN, L 2nd**

SIT TO SIDE

1-8	**Lift torso upright kneeling POS**	**Move to V POS OVRHD**
1-8	**Sit to L side (swastika, L leg FRT, R BK)**	**Circle DWN R 2nd**
1-8	**Lift torso to upright kneeling POS**	**Move to V POS OVRHD**
1-8	**Sit to R side, end lying on R side (sliding R HND to FLR as you lay-out)**	**End in V POS OVRHD (Do no rest HD on arms; frame HD with arms)**

Jackknife Contraction

1-8	**Jackknife contraction (close FT to HNDS, keeping knees and elbows locked)**	**HNDS end holding FT**

JACKKNIFE

1-8	**Open to arched POS (bending BK, controlled)**	**V POS OVRHD**
1-4	**Close to jackknife contraction (diminish 4 CTS)**	**HNDS end holding FT**
5-8	**Open to arched POS**	**V POS OVRHD**
1-2	**Jackknife CON (diminish 2 CTS)**	**HNDS at FT**
3-4	**Open to arched POS**	**V POS OVRHD**
1	**Jackknife CON (diminish 1 CT)**	**At FT**
2	**Open arch**	**V POS OVRHD**
3-8	**RPT jackknife 3 Xs**	**Same as above**
1-16	**CON and relax to fetal POS, lying on R side**	**At knees**

1-8	Open to arched POS with L leg BK—arabesque	V POS OVRHD

ARABESQUE LYING ON SIDE

1-8	CON to fetal POS on R side and lift torso to upright kneeling POS	Move to V POS OVRHD

SIDE FETAL POSITION

1-8	Sit to L side, end lying on L side (sliding L HND to FLR as you lay-out)	End in V POS OVRHD
8,8's 1-4	RPT all jackknife CON, etc.	Same
	End kneeling, torso upright	

Lunge FWD R and Pelvis Sit

1-2	Lunge FWD R, L knee remains on FLR	2nd POS, LJA
3-4	R knee returns to kneeling POS	1st POS
5-6	Lunge R to 2nd, L knee remains on FLR	2nd POS LJA
7-8	CON pelvis and sit on FLR	2nd POS jazz HNDS
1-4	Hold sitting on FLR	LJA
5-6	CON lift pelvis on FLR	2nd POS jazz HND
7-8	Pulse to 2nd in lunge and return R knee to kneeling POS	1st
2,8's	RPT and REV lunge FWD L	Same as above
4, 8's	RPT entire lunge exercise above R and L	

Lunge FWD R and Torso Turn L

1-2	Lunge FWD R, lock L knee	2nd POS LJA
3-8	Turn torso to L side, R knee remains in bent POS, L is locked, TO and ankle flexed (you are now facing S#6)	Same
1-4	CON pelvis and sit to FLR	2nd POS jazz HNDS
5-8	Hold POS (R leg bent, L locked and extended to 2nd)	LJA
1-4	CON and lift pelvis off FLR	2nd POS jazz HNDS
5-8	Turn torso BK to FRT and place L knee on FLR	LJA
1-2	Place R knee on FLR (ahead of L)	LJA
3-4	Lift L FT off FLR (you are now perched on both knees)	LJA

5-8	Hold perch POS	LJA-BK

PERCH POSITION

1-16	Hold L instep with both HNDS, and pulse FT to BK (stretch for thighs)	Holding instep
1-8	Return L FT to FLR, and kneel with both knees together, torso upright.	1st POS
1-8	Sit buttocks on heel, HD on FLR, 1-4. CON and lift to kneeling upright, 5-8.	Same

Reverse Lunge and Torso Turn

8, 8's	RPT and REV lunge FWD L, lock R knee	

On All Fours Face To FLR (HNDS and knees on FLR)

1-8	Place HNDS on FLR, BK STR, face looking at FLR (you are now on all 4s)	HNDS on FLR under SHLS
1-2	Passe R knee to chest NTO	Same
3-4	Extend R leg to 2nd POS NTO	Same

2nd POSITION EXTENSION, NTO

5-6	Passe R knee to chest NTO	Same
7-8	Extend R leg to arabesque TO	Same
1-2	Passe R knee to chest NTO	Same
3-4	Developpe R leg FWD	Move to fingertips, as you need the space for the FWD extension
5-8	Passe R to chest and return R knee to FLR	Same
2, 8's	RPT and REV, passe L knee to chest	Same
4, 8's	RPT above R and L. This time coordinate identical arm and leg (R arm and R leg)	Arm follows line of leg

Back Arches

1-8	Walk out on HNDS and lie on stomach	
1-8	The Snake—keep pelvis and legs on FLR, arch BK	Push with palms (next to pelvis) lock elbows

THE SNAKE

1-4	Return to FLR	
1-12	RPT Snake above	Same
1-4	Arch BK (lift chest and legs off FLR, swan dive)	Arms 2nd LJA
5-8	Hold	Same
1-2	Hold	Fold R arm to small of BK
3-4	Hold	Fold L arm to small of BK, hold arms together
5-8	Bend knees and fold legs to ceiling	Hold

ARCH WITH BENT KNEES

1-4	Arch back as high as possible	While opening arms and legs
5-8	Hold on FLR	
3, 8's	RPT from swan off of FLR	Same

On All Fours (Knees Off FLR) Inverted V POS

1-16	Relax—lying on stomach, turn HD to side	HNDS by SHLS
1-8	Walk on HNDS, to inverted V POS (HNDS and FT on FLR, buttocks to ceiling)	Palms supporting, lock elbows
2, 8's	RPT passe combination, done in previous all fours section with knees on FLR, working R leg (leg 2nd, arabesque and FWD)	Same

LEG EXTENSION 2nd
FROM INVERTED V

2, 8's	Passe combination, working L leg	Same
1-8	Walk out on HNDS to lying on FLR on stomach	Same
1-16	Relax—hold POS	

Stretch for Feet and Arabesque Penche

1-8	Walk HNDS back to inverted V POS, HNDS and FT on FLR, buttocks to ceiling	Palms supporting, lock elbows
1-4	Lift FT and on to PTS of toes	Same
5-8	Roll to FRT of instep, flex knees slightly (stretch instep)	

1-4	Lift FT and on to PTS again	
5-8	Flex toes and stretch heels to FLR	
1-16	RPT above stretch for FT	
1-8	Passe R knee to chest, and stretch to arabesque (TO)	Same
1-8	Hold arabesque (lift leg as high as possible, lay-out FWD	2nd POS LJA

ARABESQUE LAY-OUT FORWARD

1-8	Passe R leg into chest and DWN to FLR	
3, 8's	RPT and REV L leg passe, arabesque	Palms on FLR
1-8	Walk out on HNDS to lying on FLR on stomach	Palms on FLR
1-16	Relax—hold POS	

Knee Hinges

1-8	Walk on HNDS and kneel on both knees, 2nd PP	Palms on FLR
1-8	Slow knee hinge (keep straight line from knees thru pelvis, thru BK to SHLS). Stretch is for strengthening thighs. Hinge until SHLS touch FLR.	2nd POS, LJA

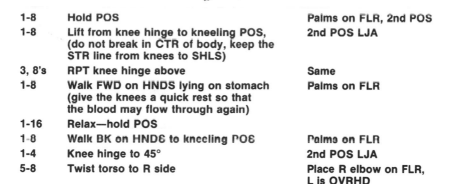

LAY-OUT KNEE HINGE

1-8	Hold POS	Palms on FLR, 2nd POS
1-8	Lift from knee hinge to kneeling POS, (do not break in CTR of body, keep the STR line from knees to SHLS)	2nd POS LJA
3, 8's	RPT knee hinge above	Same
1-8	Walk FWD on HNDS lying on stomach (give the knees a quick rest so that the blood may flow through again)	Palms on FLR
1-16	Relax—hold POS	
1-8	Walk BK on HNDS to kneeling POS	Palms on FLR
1-4	Knee hinge to 45°	2nd POS LJA
5-8	Twist torso to R side	Place R elbow on FLR, L is OVRHD

1-4	Hold side POS, do not REL buttocks	Same
5-8	Return to 45° knee hinge	2nd POS LJA
1-4	Arch BK, drop HD	Drop elbows and open arms BK

ARCH AND BACK BEND
FROM 45° KNEE HINGE

5-8	Lift torso to kneeling POS and sit on FLR between FT	1st POS
1-8	Walk out on HNDS to lying on FLR on stomach	Palms on FLR
1-16	Relax—hold POS	
1-8	Walk BK on HNDS to kneeling POS	Palms on FLR
4, 8's	RPT knee hinge to 45°—twist torso L	Same

V POSITION SIT, ATTITUDE, BATTEMENT
—Floor Progression No. 1

Start lying on FLR, on BK   Arms OVRHD

COUNTS	BODY MOVEMENT	ARMS
1-8	Swing to V POS sit, and hold POS	Arms OVRHD, V POS
1-2	Turn torso R, face S#8, R leg bends at knee FWD of pelvis and rests on FLR	2nd POS LJA
3-4	L leg swings to FRT attitude, still face S#8	Same

FRONT ATTITUDE

5-8	Hold POS	Press jazz HNDS to 4th POS, R HND OVRHD, L to 2nd
1-4	Swing body FRT, CON pelvis, rib-cage and HD, knees into chest. PT toes, heels off FLR	HNDS holding knees
5-8	Open to V POS sit	V POS OVRHD
1-8	REV and turn torso L (R FRT attitude)	LJA & press jazz HNDS 4th
1-8	RPT body FRT, CON and open to V	Hold knees, then V POS OVRHD
1-2	RPT—turn torso R, face S#8, R leg bends at knee, FWD of pelvis, and rests on FLR	2nd POS LJA
3-4	L leg swings to attitude 2nd, off FLR, still face S#8	Same

5-8	Hold POS	Press jazz HNDS to 4th POS, R HND OVRHD, L to 2nd
1-8	RPT—body FRT, CON and open to V	Hold knees, then V POS OVRHD
1-8	REV and turn torso L (R attitude 2nd)	LJA and press jazz HNDS 4th
1-8	RPT—body FRT, CON and open to V	Hold knees, then V POS OVRHD
1-2	Turn torso R, face S#8, R leg bends on FLR	2nd POS LJA
3-4	L leg swings to BK attitude (off FLR)	Same
5-8	Hold POS	Press wrists to V POS, FRT of chest
1-8	RPT body FRT, CON and open to V	Hold knees, then V POS OVRHD
1-8	REV and turn torso L (R BK attitude)	Press wrists FWD
1-8	RPT body FRT, CON and open to V	Hold knees, then V POS OVRHD
1-16	Slow contraction of pelvis, rib-cage and HD and descend to FLR	2nd POS jazz HNDS

V POSITION SIT
—Floor Progression No. 2
(Holding V POS Sit 8 CTS)

Lying on FLR on BK   Arms V POS OVRHD

COUNTS	BODY MOVEMENT	ARMS
1-8	Swing from FLR to V POS sit—hold	V POS OVRHD
1-8	Twist torso R and sit swastika POS (R leg FRT, L BK)	LJA

SWASTIKA SIT

1-8	Return to V POS sit FRT—hold	V POS OVRHD
1-8	Twist torso L and sit swastika POS (R leg FRT, L BK)	LJA
1-8	Return to V POS sit FRT—hold	V POS OVRHD
1-8	Twist torso R, R leg on FLR (knee bent), L attitude 2nd off FLR NTO	ILJA

ATTITUDE SECOND

| 1-8 | Return to V POS sit FRT—hold | V POS OVRHD |
| 1-8 | Twist torso L, L leg on FLR (knee bent) R attitude 2nd off FLR NTO | ILJA |

1-8	Return to V POS sit FRT—hold	V POS OVRHD
1-4	Twist torso R, R leg on FLR (knee bent) L attitude 2nd off FLR NTO	V POS OVRHD
5-8	Extend L to 2nd NTO (off FLR)	Circle both arms FRT of chest and open 2nd LJA
1-4	Slide to FLR on R side, FT together	R HND supports body during slide to FLR

SLIDE TO SIDE

5-8	Roll L on BK to L side and sit up to POS with R leg attitude 2nd (off FLR)	V POS OVRHD
1-4	Hold	
5-8	Extend R to 2nd NTO (off FLR)	Circle both arms FRT of chest and open 2nd LJA
1-4	Slide to FLR on L side, FT together	L HND supports body during slide to FLR
1-24	RPT roll over R, hold, extension, slide. RPT roll over L, hold, extension, slide.	Same
1-8	Lying on BK, swing up to V POS sit. Hold.	V POS OVRHD
1-16	CON pelvis, rib-cage, HD and descend to FLR slowly	2nd POS jazz HNDS

CONTRACTION TO FLOOR

Swing up from FLR and RPT entire stretch from beginning.

KNEE HINGE FLOOR PROGRESSION

Kneeling 2nd POS   Torso upright   Arms 1st POS

COUNTS	BODY MOVEMENT	ARMS
1-8	Lie BK until SHLS on FLR	2nd POS LJA
1-8	Relax (don't tense body)—hold POS on FLR	2nd POS, palms on FLR
1-8	Lift with arched BK, return to upright kneeling POS	V POS BK

"Stretching must be done faithfully and vigorously."

All Fours

1-8	All 4s on FLR (face to FLR) TBTP BK — 5-8 walk up to inverted V POS (buttocks to ceiling, knees locked)	Palms on FLR
1-8	Passe R knee to chest and extend to arabesque TO	Same

ARABESQUE FROM INVERTED V POSITION

1-8	Passe R knee to chest and extend 2nd POS NTO	Same
1-8	Slide R leg to FLR 2nd POS TO, end in FWD split	Palms on FLR FRT of pelvis
1-8	Pulse in FWD split	Same
1-8	Place elbows on FLR and lie on stomach, legs remain in 2nd TO	Palms and elbows on FLR FWD of chest
1-8	Make diamond shape of legs (FT together, knees apart)	Palms on FLR next to SHLS
1-8	Lift torso off FLR from above POS	Push with palms, lock elbows
1-8	Hold POS off FLR	Hold
1-8	Lower to torso on FLR and close legs to 1st POS, knees locked	Palms next to SHLS
1-8	Return to all 4s (face to FLR)	Palms on FLR
1-8	Lift to kneeling POS, torso upright	2nd POS LJA
1-4	45° knee hinge (do not touch FLR)	2nd LJA
5-8	Twist torso R and place R elbow and palm on FLR	L arm OVRHD

TORSO TWIST—ELBOW ON FLOOR

1-4	Return FRT to 45° knee hinge	2nd POS LJA
5-8	Accent BK BD and lift to upright POS	Elbows pull BK and end in V POS BK
1-16	RPT and REV above 16 CTS, twist torso L	Same
6,8's	RPT above from all 4s (use L leg arabesque)	Same

ON ALL FOURS FACE TO CEILING
—Floor Progression

HNDS and FT on FLR   Face parallel to ceiling
Torso and pelvis in STR line from SHLS and knees (TBTP)

COUNTS	BODY MOVEMENT	ARMS
1-8	**FT parallel 2nd POS, HNDS under SHLS —hold POS**	**HNDS on FLR**
1-2	**Bring R knee into chest**	**Same**
3-4	**Developpe R leg to ceiling**	**Same**

ALL FOURS—DEVELOPPE LEG

5-6	**Return R knee to chest**	**Same**
7-8	**Place R FT on FLR**	**Same**
1-8	**REV—use L leg for developpe**	**Same**
1-4	**Buttocks sits on FLR**	**Same**
5-8	**Hold**	**Shake wrists (circulation)**
1-8	**Return to TBTP POS—hold POS**	**HNDS on FLR**
1-4	**Developpe R leg to ceiling**	**Same**
5-8	**Cross R leg over L, placing R FT on FLR, FRT of L (knees locked, sous-sus POS)**	**Body weight is supported by L HND, elbow locked, R arm extended to ceiling**
1-8	**Developpe R leg 2nd POS, TO**	**Same**
1-4	**Bring R leg into neutral passe POS**	**Same**
5-8	**Developpe R leg FWD**	**Same**
1-8	**Ronde de jambe R leg and return to all fours POS (face to ceiling)**	**R arm swings thru 2nd and place R HND on FLR**
1-8	**RET to sitting POS**	**Shake wrists**
10,8's	**REV and RPT all CTS above, using L leg for developpe**	

Jazz Barre

JAZZ BARRE (Standing At Barre)

A knowledge of classical ballet terminology and technique is a prerequisite for a jazz barre. Therefore only intermediate and advanced students of jazz are offered this course. Jazz barre may also be used center floor with minor adjustments.

Plie Series

Begin 2nd POS, L HND Barre

COUNTS	BODY MOVEMENT	ARMS
1-4	Hold	
5-8	Hold	Lift R V POS OVRHD
1-4	Grande-plie AST ISOL RC L	Pull R elbow DWN

GRANDE PLIE 2nd
ISOLATION RIB-CAGE

5-8	Lock knees AST ISOL RC R	Lift R elbow up
1-8	RPT	
1	FT parallel 2nd, lift torso	R V POS OVRHD
2-4	TBTP torso FWD	
5-8	Drop torso DWN FWD	R HND R ankle
1-8	CON torso upright	R V POS OVRHD
1-4	Tabletop lay-out BK	R wrist press FWD

TABLETOP LAY-OUT BACK

5-8	Recover torso	R V POS OVRHD
1	FT TO 2nd POS	R V POS OVRHD
2-4	Releve half-toe TO	Add L V POS OVRHD
5-8	Balance	Both V POS OVRHD
1-2	FT TO half-toe 2nd, CON pelvis	V POS OVRHD, flex wrists

ON HALF-TOE,
CONTRACT PELVIS

3-4	Neutral pelvis	V POS OVRHD
5-8	RPT	
1-2	RPT CON	
3-6	Lower heels, locked knees, contracted pelvis	V POS OVRHD, flexed wrists
7-8	Demi-plie 2nd TO, 1st POS TO	2nd POS
1-64	RPT all (1st POS), change 4th POS	
1-48	RPT 48 CTS — plie series 4th POS	
1-7	Balance arabesque POS	V POS OVRHD

ARABESQUE BALANCE

8	5th POS demi-plie	DWN
1-48	RPT 48 CTS — plie series 5th POS	
1-4	Passe R TO, L releve balance	V POS OVRHD
5-8	Hold passe balance	
1-4	Lower L heel AST bend torso R and plie L	Same

SIDE STRETCH & PASSE

5-8	Hold POS	
1-4	Recover torso upright AST develope R 2nd POS	2nd POS, LJA
5-6	Hold extension	
7-8	R X L turn and RPT facing opposite side RPT all L	

"Aerobic refers to anything that shoots healthy oxygen through body and brain, like dance stretches and limbering."

Tendu Series

Begin 5th POS R FT FWD, lock
L HND on Barre

COUNTS	BODY MOVEMENT	ARMS
1	**Tendu R FWD TO**	**LJA 2nd**

TENDU FORWARD

2-7	**Rotate R in-out, locked knee**	
8	**5th POS TO, locked knees**	**DWN**
1-24	**RPT en croix (2nd POS, BK, and RPT 2nd POS)**	
1	**Tendu R FWD TO**	**LJA 2nd**
2	**Press R heel DWN, locked knee**	
3	**Lift R heel, locked knee**	
4-7	**RPT CTS 2-3**	
8	**5th POS TO, locked knees**	**DWN**
1-24	**RPT en croix (2nd POS, BK, and RPT 2nd POS)**	
1	**Tendu R FWD TO**	**LJA 2nd**
2	**Demi-plie 4th POS TO**	

DEMI-PLIE 4th

3	**Releve 4th POS TO**	
4-5	**RPT CTS 2-3**	
6	**Demi-plie 4th POS TO**	
7	**Tendu R FWD TO, locked knees**	
8	**R 5th POS TO**	**DWN**
1-24	**RPT en croix (2nd POS, BK, and RPT 2nd POS)**	
1	**Tendu R FWD TO**	**LJA 2nd**
2-3	**Rotate R in-out, locked knees**	
4-5	**Press R heel DWN, lift R heel up**	

| 6 | Demi-plie 4th POS TO |
| 7 | Sous-sus 5th POS |

SOUS-SUS (5th)

8	Plie 5th POS TO
1-24	RPT en croix (2nd POS, BK, and RPT 2nd POS)
Same	RPT all above starting with L tendu	Same

Rond de Jambe Series

Begin 5th POS   R FT FRT   L HND Barre

COUNTS	BODY MOVEMENT	ARMS
1	Tap R FWD, locked knee, TO	LJA 2nd
2	Tap 2nd	
3	Tap BK	
4	Tap 2nd	
5-8	REV, begin BK	
1-8	RPT	
&1	R 1st POS and FWD	
&2	Circle R 2nd, close R 1st (rond de jambe en de hors)	

CIRCLE R 2nd

&3-8	RPT 3 Xs
&1-8	REV circle BK (rond de jambe en dedans)
1-4	RPT rond de jambe en de hors 2 Xs
5-8	RPT rond de jambe en de das 2 Xs
1-2	Rond de jambe en de hors 1 X
3-4	Rond de jambe en de dans 1 X
5-8	RPT above 4 CTS

1	Battement R 2nd POS
2-5	Rond de jambe en l'air en dehors 2 Xs
6	Plie L, R 2nd POS en l'air

CIRCLE EN L'AIR

7	Sous-sus 5th POS, R BK
8	Plie 5th POS
1-8	RPT rond de jambe en de dans en l'air
1-16	RPT above 16 CTS
Same	RPT all L

Frappe

Begin R Sur le Cou de Pied
(R Heel to L Ankle—Flex FT)
L HND Barre

SUR LE COU DE PIED

COUNTS	BODY MOVEMENT	ARMS
1	Frappe (brush) R FWD	LJA 2nd
2	Demi-plie 4th POS TO	
3	Lock L knee, tendu R above FLR	
4	5th POS TO	DWN
5-16	RPT en croix	
1	Frappe (brush) R FWD	LJA 2nd

FRAPPE

2	R cou de pied flexed	
3	R passe PTD TO, L releve	
4	R cou de pied, X BK L	
5-8	REV above 4 CTS	
1	Frappe R 2nd POS	
2	R cou de pied, X BK L	
3-8	REV and RPT	DWN CT 8

1-4	**Passe R TO, developpe FWD**	**LJA 2nd**
5-6	**Grand rond de jambe 2nd POS TO**	
7-8	**Arabesque**	
1-2	**Attitude R, releve plie L, TBTP torso,** **face parallel to FLR**	**R arm DWN**

TABLETOP ATTITUDE

3-4	**Arabesque R, lock L, lower heel**	**R arm FWD**
5-8	**RPT above 4 CTS**	
1-8	**Releve L, R arabesque, balance**	**R FWD, L 2nd**
Same	**RPT all L**	**Same**

Hip Isolations

Begin 1st POS NTO   L HND Barre

COUNTS	BODY MOVEMENT	ARMS
1	**1st POS "plie-releve" NTO**	**JH 2nd**

"PLIE-RELEVE" 1st POSITION

2-6	**ISOL hip R-L on beat**	
7	**Neutral hip**	
8	**Lock knees AST lower heels**	**DWN**
1	**R FWD NTO 4th POS "plie-releve"**	**JH 2nd**

"PLIE-RELEVE" 4th POSITION

2-6	**CON and REL pelvis on beat**	
7	**Neutral pelvis**	
8	**1st POS NTO**	**DWN**

1	**R passe NTO**	**JH 2nd**
2-4	**Step R 4th POS NTO, AST triple hip** **R-L-R on beat (rock style)**	

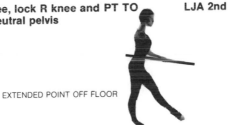

TRIPLE HIP ISOLATION

5-8	**REV BK**	
1-8	**RPT triple hip jazz style (opposition)**	
Same	**RPT all L**	**Same**

Contraction and Release Series

COUNTS	BODY MOVEMENT	ARMS
1-2	**Tendu R FWD TO**	**LJA 2nd**
3-4	**Plie L, AST flex R knee and FT TO,** **CON pelvis**	**JH 2nd**

FLEX KNEE AND ANKLE

5-6	**Lock L knee, lock R knee and PT TO** **off FLR, neutral pelvis**	**LJA 2nd**

EXTENDED POINT OFF FLOOR

7	**Tendu R FLR TO**	
8	**5th POS TO**	**DWN**
1-24	**RPT en croix**	
1-2	**Tendu R FWD TO**	**LJA 2nd**
3-4	**Plie L, AST flex R knee and FT TO** **—release torso and HD**	**LJA 2nd, palm up**
5-6	**Lock L knee, lock R knee and PT TO** **off FLR, neutral torso and HD**	**LJA 2nd**

7	Tendu R TO FLR	
8	5th POS TO	DWN
1-24	RPT en croix	
1-2	Tendu R FWD TO	LJA 2nd
3-4	Plie, flex, and CON AST	JH 2nd

PLIE, FLEX, CONTRACT

5-6	Lock knees and REL torso and HD AST	LJA 2nd
7	Tendu R FWD TO	
8	5th POS TO	DWN
1-24	RPT en croix	
Same	RPT all L	Same
	The above may also be done with the supporting leg in "plie-releve" on CTS 3-6.	

Tabletop—Knees—Knee Hinge

Begin parallel 2nd, NTO, lock
L HND Barre

COUNTS	BODY MOVEMENT	ARMS
1-4	TBTP torso FWD	V POS OVRHD
5-6	Demi-plie NTO	

TABLETOP TORSO,
DEMI-PLIE

7-8	Lock knees	
1-8	Body roll (plie, push pelvis FWD, REL BK, recover)	R DWN, BK, and OVRHD
1-2	TBTP torso FWD	V POS OVRHD
3-4	Demi-plie NTO	
5-6	Both knees FLR AST 45° lay-out	2nd LJA

45° KNEE HINGE,
KNEES ON FLOOR

7-8	Hold	
1-2	Return TBTP demi-plie, NTO	**V POS OVRHD**
3-4	Lock knees	
5-8	Body roll	
1-32	RPT above except knee hinge, knees are off FLR	

45° KNEE HINGE, KNEES OFF FLOOR

Same	RPT all L	Same

Battement Series

Begin 5th POS TO, R FT FRT
L HND Barre

COUNTS	BODY MOVEMENT	ARMS
1	Tendu R FWD TO	LJA 2nd
2	Demi-plie 4th POS TO	
3	Battement L BK PTD, R locked	

BATTEMENT, BACK POINT

4	L 5th POS BK locked	
5	Tendu L BK TO	
6	Demi-plie 4th POS TO	
7	Battement R FWD PTD, L locked	
8	R 5th POS locked	
1	Battement R 2nd PTD, AST demi-plie L	
2	5th POS R BK, locked knees	
3	Battement R 2nd PTD, AST demi-plie L	
&4	5th POS R FWD, locked knees	
5-8	RPT above 4 CTS	
1	Tendu R FWD TO	LJA 2nd
2	Demi-plie 4th POS TO	
3	Battement L BK PTD, releve R AST	
4	5th POS demi-plie	
5-8	REV	

1	**Battement R 2nd PTD, AST plie-releve L**
2	**5th POS R BK, locked knees**
3-8	**REV and RPT**
	Also done with a flexed FT on the battement leg

FLEX BATTEMENT

Same	**RPT all L**	**Same**

Attitude with Shoulder and Rib-Cage Isolations

Begin 5th POS, R FT FWD
L HND on Barre

COUNTS	BODY MOVEMENT	ARMS
1	**R attitude FWD TO**	**LJA 2nd**
2	**Hold attitude, AST ISOL R SHL FWD**	

FORWARD ATTITUDE
AND SHOULDER ISOLATION

3	**Developpe R FWD, AST ISOL L SHL FWD**	

LEG EXTENDED FORWARD
AND SHOULDER ISOLATION

4	**5th POS**	**DWN**

"Don't do anything that strains."

5-16	**RPT en croix**	
1	**R attitude FWD TO**	**LJA 2nd**
2	**Hold attitude, AST ISOL RC R**	
3	**Developpe R FWD, AST ISOL RC L**	
4	**5th POS**	
5-16	**RPT en croix**	

SECOND ATTITUDE AND ISOLATION

SECOND LEG EXTENDED AND ISOLATION

Same	**RPT all L**	**Same**

Jazz Barre Stretch No. 1

Begin R Ankle on Barre Body Facing Leg (R DIAG)
Arms 1st

COUNTS	BODY MOVEMENT	ARMS
1-8	**Pulse body FWD over leg**	**Both HNDS around R FT**
1-2	**Plie L, AST pull body close R leg**	**Same**

PLIE—BODY OVER LEG

3-4	**Look L, hold torso close R leg**	**Same**
5-8	**RPT**	
1-8	**Side stretch inside (face wall)**	**V POS OVRHD**

SIDE STRETCH INSIDE

1-8	Side stretch outside (face room)	L HND R FT, R V POS OVRHD

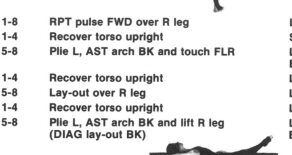

SIDE STRETCH OUTSIDE

1-8	RPT pulse FWD over R leg	L HND barre, R V POS OVRHD
1-4	Recover torso upright	Same
5-8	Plie L, AST arch BK and touch FLR	L HND barre, R DWN and BK and OVRHD
1-4	Recover torso upright	L HND barre, R OVRHD
5-8	Lay-out over R leg	L HND barre, R OVRHD
1-4	Recover torso upright	L HND barre, R OVRHD
5-8	Plie L, AST arch BK and lift R leg (DIAG lay-out BK)	L HND barre, R DWN and BK and OVRHD

LAY-OUT BACK

1-4	Recover torso upright, hold R leg extended FWD	L HND barre, R 2nd LJA
5-8	Grande rond de jambe arabesque R	Same
1-8	Balance, L releve, R arabesque	L OVRHD, R FWD
10, 8's	RPT and REV all L	Same

Jazz Barre Stretch No. 2

Begin Standing L, Face Barre with
R FT FWD on Barre between both HNDS

COUNTS	BODY MOVEMENT	ARMS
1-4	Flex R knee NTO, AST pulse TWD barre	HNDS on barre
5-8	Lock R knee, HD DWN on knee	Same
1-24	RPT 3 Xs	
1-4	Turn torso L, R. 2nd POS on barre	LJA 2nd
5-8	TBTP torso FWD	V POS OVRHD

TABLETOP TORSO FORWARD

1-4	Torso over L leg	HNDS ankle
5-8	Pulse torso TWD L LEG	Wrap L leg
1-2	Plie L, hold torso in place	HNDS hold ankle

PLIE—HOLD ANKLE

3-4	Lock L, hold torso in place	Same
5-8	RPT	
1-4	TBTP torso FWD	V POS OVRHD
5-8	Recover torso upright	Same
1-4	Turn torso L facing out, R arabesque on barre	Same
5-8	Plie L, AST arch BK TWD barre	V POS OVRHD TWD barre
1-4	Lock L, recover torso upright	Same
5-8	TBTP FWD	V POS OVRHD
1-4	Torso DWN over L leg	HNDS FLR
5-8	Lift R leg ceiling	Same

LEG TO CEILING

1-2	Plie L, AST flex R knee and FT TO	Same
3-4	Lock L, AST stretch R TWD ceiling	Same
5-8	RPT	
1-4	TBTP torso FWD	V POS OVRHD
5-8	Torso upright, R arabesque	LJA 2nd
1-4	Turn torso R, R 2nd POS barre	Same
5-8	Turn torso face barre, R FWD barre	Same
1-2	Lift R off barre	HNDS barre
3-4	Rond de jambe 2nd	Same
5-6	Rond de jambe arabesque	Same
7-8	R DWN	Same
Same	REV all with L leg on barre	Same

"Dizzy? Quit, rest, and start again.
(Keep eyes open.)"

Center Barre

HEAD POSITIONS AND PORT DE BRAS
—Floor Progressions

Square POS standing   RT toe PTD BK   Arms 1st

SQUARE POSITION

COUNTS	BODY MOVEMENT	ARMS
1 (Slow)	**NEUTRAL POS—HD FRT, long neck, focus eyes FWD, above eye level**	**V POS FRT of chest (palms parallel)**

HEAD—NEUTRAL POSITION
ARMS—V POSITION FRONT

| **2** | **DIAG POS—turn HD and spot C#1** | **V POS OVRHD** |

HEAD—DIAGONAL POSITION
ARMS—V POSITION OVERHEAD

| **3** | **PROFILE POS—turn HD and spot S#8 (chin up)** | **ILJA—2nd** |

HEAD—PROFILE POSITION
ARMS—INVERTED LONG JAZZ
ARM 2nd POSITION

| **4** | **SIDE STRETCH POS—HD tilts R (stretch L side muscle, focus eyes FWD)** | **L HND at L pelvis, R HND circles into SHL and wrist presses to 2nd** |

HEAD—SIDE STRETCH
ARMS—WRIST PRESS 2nd

| **5** | **RELEASE POS—tilt HD up, focus FWD** | **ILJA** |

HEAD—RELEASE POSITION
ARMS—INVERTED LONG JAZZ
ARM 2nd POSITION

COUNTS	BODY MOVEMENT	ARMS

6 CONTRACT POS—tilt HD DWN, focus FWD

LJA (elbows high)

HEAD—CONTRACT POSITION
ARMS—LONG JAZZ ARMS
2nd POSITION

&7 HEAD SWING—swing L to R, focus FWD

Palms on pelvis

HEAD—SWINGS LEFT TO RIGHT
ARMS—FISTS AT PELVIS

&8 HEAD SWING—swing R to L, focus FWD

Same

HEAD—SWINGS RIGHT TO LEFT
ARMS—FISTS AT PELVIS

9 & 10 HEAD CIRCLE—circle HD R, end with accent R

R arm circles to 2nd, BK, OVRHD and 2nd

HEAD—CIRCLE R
ARMS—CIRCLE R ARM
OVERHEAD AND 2nd

11 & 12 HEAD CIRCLE—circle HD L, end with accent L

L arm circles to 2nd, BK, OVRHD and 2nd

HEAD—CIRCLE L
ARMS—CIRCLE LEFT ARM
OVERHEAD AND 2nd

13,14	**Return HD to square POS**	**2nd LJA**
15,16	**Hold square (HD DWN)**	**Press to 1st**
1-16	**REV—start neutral and on CT 2 focus L DIAG**	**Same**

NOTE: Exercise may also be done with jazz walk forward, coordinating arms and head positions above. On head circles, 9 & 10, 11 & 12, feet are doing triples (R, L, R and L, R, L) and walk R, L, R, L on counts 13 through 16. Start coordination with arms and feet, add head later.

DEVELOPPE COMBINATION—MOVING ACROSS FLOOR

CB, standing   L FT FWD, locked knee   R toe PTD BK
Arms 1st POS on pelvis
These are high extension kicks; try for OVRHD zenith.

DEVELOPPE AND PLIE—
RELEVE POSITION

COUNTS	BODY MOVEMENT	ARMS
1	Step R FWD, plie NTO	2nd LJA
2	Developpe L, kick FRT, "plie-releve" POS supporting leg	Same
3	Step L FWD, plie NTO, R passe BK TO	Both HNDS to SHLS
4	Releve L, developpe R, 2nd POS	V POS OVRHD
5	Step pique R (on half toe, locked knee) face S#6, L low arabesque TO	HNDS to SHLS
6	"Plie-releve" POS R, L lifts to high arabesque (torso parallel to FLR)	4th POS L pushes FRT, R 2nd, flex wrists
7-8	Turn L, stepping L, R (pique), end facing FRT	Circle OVRHD, X chest and open 2nd LJA
1-8	RPT and REV above step L FWD	Same
1-32	RPT R and L across FLR 2 Xs	Same

DEVELOPPE AND BACK LAY-OUT

CB   Demi-plie 1st POS NTO   CON torso and HD   Arms 1st
Face C#2 and travel diagonally to C#1. After 4 CTS,
change direction and travel to C#2.

COUNTS	BODY MOVEMENT	ARMS
1	Step R PP 2nd NTO (face C#2)	2nd POS LJA
2	XLOR plie	Cross FRT of chest, fists
3	Step R PP 2nd plie	2nd POS LJA
&4	Releve R on "&" CT, passe L NTO "Plie-releve" POS R leg, extend L to C#2, torso lay-out BK	R HND to SHL on "&" CT, L 2nd, thrust R HND to C#2
5-8	Change direction, face C#1, RPT and REV above, step L PP 2nd	Same
1-8	RPT above R and L	Same

TORSO LAY-OUT BACK,
"PLIE-RELEVE" SUPPORTING LEG

GRANDE PLIE 2nd POSITION
AND SERIES OF DEVELOPPES

CB 1st POS NTO   Locked knees   Arms 1st

COUNTS	BODY MOVEMENT	ARMS
1-4	Step R 2nd grande plie	Circle OVRHD and jazz HNDS 2nd CTS 1,3 — place HNDS on pelvis CT 4
5-6	Passe R to knee TO, developpe to C#1 L holds plie	Circle R HND to SHL and push palm FRT
7-8	Passe R to knee TO, developpe	Place R on pelvis, L jazz HND stretches on 2nd
1-2	Passe R knee TO and BK to BK attitude TO	Place L on pelvis, R jazz HND stretches OVRHD
3-4	Hold R instep with L HND—BK	R lifts to C#1
5-6	Hold POS and lock L knee	Hold POS
7-8	Passe R TO (face FRT on locked knee)	2nd POS jazz HNDS
1-4	Developpe R 2nd, flex ankle on CT 4	Hold
5-8	Lift leg from hip socket (4 pulses)	Hold
1-4	Rond de jambe R to arabesque, PT toes	2nd POS LJA
5-6	Brush battement R FWD, L knee locked	Same
7-8	Lunge deep R FWD, and close R to L 1st PP	Move to 1st POS
4,8's	RPT and REV above step L, 2nd grande plie	Same

DEVELOPPE TO C#1

LEG SWINGS PROGRESSION

CB 5th POS TO   R FT FRT, knees locked
Lift arms 1st to 2nd LJA 4 CTS before starting exercise.

COUNTS	BODY MOVEMENT	ARMS
1-2	Brush R attitude C#2, close R 5th on CT 2, L knee locked, flat FT	2nd POS LJA
3-4	Brush R attitude 2nd POS, close 5th CT 4	Same
5-8	RPT as above, plie 2nd POS on CT 8	Same—arms 1st on CT 8

Counts	Body Movement	Arms
1-8	Brush L attitude C#1, close L 5th on CT 2, RPT remaining CTS, plie 2nd on 8	Same—arms 1st CT 8
1-8	RPT attitude swings R, plie CTS 2,4,6,8	Same—arms 1st CT 8
1-8	RPT attitude swings L with plies	Same—arms 1st CT 8
1-8	RPT attitude swings R (releve and plie), releve CT 1, plie CT 2, etc.	Same—arms 1st CT 8
1-8	RPT attitude swings L, releve and plie	Same—arms 1st CT 8
6, 8's	RPT as above with leg swings FWD and 2nd	Same as above

BRUSH ATTITUDE 2nd POSITION

LEG SWINGS AND CIRCLE PROGRESSION

CB 5th POS TO R FRT, knees locked
Lift arms 1st to 2nd LJA 4 CTS before starting exercise.

COUNTS	BODY MOVEMENT	ARMS
1-2	Brush R attitude circle L to R, close 5th R FRT	2nd POS LJA

BRUSH ATTITUDE
TURNED-OUT, LEFT

3-4	Brush R attitude circle R to L, close 5th FRT	Same
5-6	Brush R attitude circle L to R, close 5th FRT	Same
7-8	Brush R attitude 2nd, grande plie 2nd on CT 8	1st on CT 8

GRANDE PLIE, 2nd

1-8	RPT and REV above, brush L attitude —circle R to L—continue	Same

| 1-8 | Attitude circles R, plie CTS 2,4,6,8 | Same |

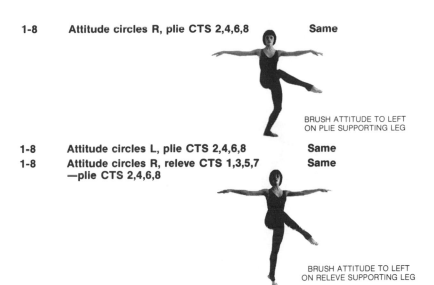

BRUSH ATTITUDE TO LEFT
ON PLIE SUPPORTING LEG

| 1-8 | Attitude circles L, plie CTS 2,4,6,8 | Same |
| 1-8 | Attitude circles R, releve CTS 1,3,5,7 —plie CTS 2,4,6,8 | Same |

BRUSH ATTITUDE TO LEFT
ON RELEVE SUPPORTING LEG

| 1-8 | Attitude circles L, RPT releve, plie above | Same |

Circles may also be done with figure 8 motion (circle L to R, close 5th BK, circle R to L, close 5th FRT)

SIT, ROLL BACK TO NECK, ROLL FORWARD AND STAND

CB   Exercise is done without using support of the HNDS —
1st PP   Knees locked   Arms 1st

COUNTS	BODY MOVEMENT	ARMS
1-2	Sit buttocks on FLR	1st POS
3-4	CON and roll up to neck vertebrae	HNDS hold knees
5-6	Roll FWD, FT 1st PP on FLR, CT 6	Same
7	Push off FLR using FT (not ankles)	1st POS (do not push with palms on FLR, legs must do pushing)
8	Stand upright, knees locked	Same
3,8's	RPT above 3 Xs	
1-8	RPT all and on CT 7 plie for leap in 1st POS, toes PTD (in air on "&" CT of 7, land plie 1st PP on CT 8)	1st POS
3, 8's	RPT above 3 Xs	

Air tour may be added to leap.

HOLD ON NECK VERTEBRAE

TORSO PROGRESSION

CB, standing   FT 2nd POS TO   Arms at sides

COUNTS	BODY MOVEMENT	ARMS
1,2 (Slow)	**Drop torso R to TBTP L (chest parallel to FLR)**	**Arms OVRHD, V POS**

DIAGONAL TABLETOP

3-4	**REV (drop L)**	**Same**
1,2,3	**Torso drop R to TBTP, to side stretch L**	**Arms OVRHD, V POS**

SIDE STRETCH

4,5,6	**REV (drop L)**	**Same**
1,2,3,4	**Torso drop to TBTP, to side stretch L, to torso twist (twist torso to face S#8) (FT 4th POS on torso twist)**	**4th POS on torso twist, (L arm OVRHD, R 2nd POS)**

TORSO TWIST

5-8	**REV (drop L)**	**Same**
1-4	**Torso drop to TBTP, to side stretch L, to torso twist**	
5	**Lift torso to upright POS (facing S#8)**	**4th POS, L arm OVRHD, R 2nd POS**
6	**Back lay-out**	**Same**
&7	**BK bend, accent HD drop**	**Elbows pull into sides of torso**
8	**BK lay-out, face to ceiling**	**V POS BK, palms parallel**

BACK LAY-OUT

| 9,10 | Grande plie, 2nd POS | Circle into chest, and to 2nd POS, LJA |

GRANDE-PLIE 2nd

11,12	CON pelvis, rib-cage and HD, and lift to standing POS	Jazz HNDS, low 2nd
1-12	REV (drop L to R)	Same as above
1-24	RPT R and L above	Same

Knees Turned-In, Turned-Out

PT R toe 2nd, lock L   Arms 2nd LJA

COUNTS	BODY MOVEMENT	ARMS
1-2	TI R knee, L locked (heel on FLR)	2nd LJA

ISOLATION RIGHT KNEE
TURNED-IN

3-4	TO R knee, L locked	Same
5-8	REV to L	
1-8	RPT all above (lift heel off FLR)	Same
1-4	Developpe R 2nd, PT, L leg locked and releve CT 3, heel DWN CT 4	2nd jazz HNDS

DEVELOPPE RIGHT 2nd,
RELEVE LEFT—COUNT 3

5-6	Flex R ankle, L remains locked	Same
7-8	Close R FT BK 5th POS, lock	1st
1-4	Grande plie, 5th	Circle (2nd, OVRHD)
5-6	Ascend (lock knees 5th)	2nd LJA

"Moving bodies attract attention."

7-8	Tendu L 2nd, TO, lock	Same

TENDU LEFT

4,8's	REV and RPT all above L Also may be done lifting heel off FLR, CTS 1-2	Same

---

Tendu and Rib-Cage

FT 5th POS TO R FT FRT Arms 1st POS

COUNTS	BODY MOVEMENT	ARMS
1 (Slow)	**Tendu (PT) R 2nd, TO, lock**	**Lift to 2nd LJA**
2-3	**Rib-cage ISOL R side, neutral**	**Same**

TENDU AND RIB-CAGE RIGHT

4	**Close R FT BK 5th, lock**	**1st**
5-8	**REV and RPT L side**	**Same**
1-8	**RPT all above moving FWD**	**Same**
1-16	**RPT all above moving BK**	**Same**

Tendu and Rib-Cage Square

FT 5th POS TO R FT FRT Arms 1st POS

COUNTS	BODY MOVEMENT	ARMS
1 (Slow)	**Tendu (PT) R 2nd, TO, lock**	**Lift to 2nd LJA**
2,3,4,5	**ISOL rib-cage R, FRT, L, BK**	**Same**
6	**Close R FRT, 5th POS, plie, TO, RC neutral**	**1st**
7	**Battement R 2nd, flex ankle—lock L, releve**	**2nd jazz HNDS**

RIGHT BATTEMENT 2nd,
FLEX ANKLE, LEFT RELEVE

8	**Close R BK, 5th POS, plie, TO**	**1st**
1-8	**REV and RPT L**	**Same**
1-16	**RPT R and L**	**Same**

Degage and Rib-Cage Isolation

FT 5th POS TO   R FT FRT   Arms 1st POS

COUNTS	BODY MOVEMENT	ARMS
1 (Slow)	**Degage (PT and lift R FT off FLR) 2nd, TO, lock**	**2nd LJA**
2-3	**ISOL rib-cage R, L**	**Same**

DEGAGE RIGHT,
RIB CAGE RIGHT

4	**Rib-cage neutral, close R to L, 5th TO, lock, R FRT**	**1st**
5-8	**REV and RPT**	**Same**
1-8	**RPT moving FWD**	**Same**
1-16	**RPT moving BK**	**Same**

Promenade Holding Leg Second

FT 5th POS TO   R FT FRT   Arms 1st

COUNTS	BODY MOVEMENT	ARMS
1-2	**Tendu (PT) R Toe FWD, TO, lock**	**2nd POS, LJA**
3-4	**Plie both legs (keep BK STR)**	**R HND holds R instep, L arm stretches to ceiling**

RIGHT HAND HOLDS INSTEP

5-8	**Lock knees and take R leg to 2nd, TO**	**R HND holding instep, L arm OVRHD**
1-8	**Promenade turn R, lift heel and pivot on ball of L FT (knee locked), end FRT**	**Same**

PROMENADE PIVOT TURN RIGHT,
LEG 2nd POSITION

1-8	**Rond de jambe R to arabesque–penchee**	**2nd LJA**
1-2	**Battement R FWD, lock L**	**Same**

3-6	Lay-out lunge FWD	V POS OVRHD

LAY-OUT LUNGE FORWARD

7-8	Close R to L, upright	1st
4,8's	REV and RPT all to L	Same

Port de Bras, Rib-Cage Combination

FT 2nd PP, lock   Arms 1st

COUNTS	BODY MOVEMENT	ARMS
1	Hold POS	LJA R to 2nd
2	Same	Swing L OVRHD

PORT DE BRAS—SWING
LEFT ARM OVERHEAD

3	Same	Swing L 2nd, LJA
4	Same	Swing R OVRHD
5	Same	Swing L OVRHD
6	Same	Parallel pull DWN from elbows
7	Same	2nd LJA

PARALLEL PULL DOWN
FROM ELBOWS

8	Same	Press to 1st
1-8	Add rib-cage to arms: R, FRT, L, BK (CTS 1-4), REL, CON, REL, neutral (CTS 5-8)	Same as above

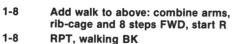

RIB CAGE RIGHT
WITH LONG JAZZ ARM RIGHT

1-8	Add walk to above: combine arms, rib-cage and 8 steps FWD, start R	Same
1-8	RPT, walking BK	Same
1-16	RPT walks FWD and BK	Same

CHOREOGRAPHED JAZZ CENTER BARRE #1
Plie Series

Begin 2nd POS TO, lock   Arms V POS OVRHD

COUNTS	BODY MOVEMENT	ARMS
1-2	Grande plie 2nd POS TO	Both X FRT body (OVRHD and DWN)

GRANDE PLIE 2nd, CROSSED ARMS

3-4	Lock knees	LJA 2nd
5-6	Grande plie	Both X FRT body (DWN and OVRHD)
7-8	Lock knees	End V POS OVRHD
1-8	RPT above 8 CTS	
1-2	Plie 2nd POS	Both DWN X FRT body
3-4	Side lunge R, L locked and PTD TO	R to S#8, L 1st

SIDE LUNGE RIGHT

5-6	Plie 2nd	Both up X FRT body
7-8	Lock knees	V POS OVRHD
1-24	REV and RPT	
1-2	Plie 2nd POS TO	Both DWN X FRT body
3-	Side lay-out R, L 2nd in air, R knee locked	R along ear, L along torso

SIDE LAY-OUT RIGHT, LEFT LEG BATTEMENT 2nd

4-6	Balance lay-out 2nd	
7	Plie	Both up X FRT body
8	Lock knees	V POS OVRHD
1-8	REV and RPT to lay-out side L	
1-16	RPT R and L above	
	Transition to 1st POS TO	
1-4	R 1st POS TO	Press DWN

| 1-2 | Demi-plie 1st POS TO | | Fists 2nd POS |
| 3-4 | Grande plie | | JH 2nd POS |

GRANDE PLIE 1st

5-6	Return demi-plie	LJA 2nd
7-8	Lock knees	DWN
1-24	RPT above 3 Xs	Same

Transition to 4th POS

| 1-2 | Tendu R FWD | Lift V POS OVRHD, palms up |

TENDU FORWARD

3-4	Press R heel DWN	Press DWN thru 4th OPP, palms DWN
1-2	Demi-plie	LJA 2nd
3-4	Grande plie	HNDS chest, elbow 2nd

GRANDE PLIE 4th POSITION

5-6	Demi-plie	Lift OVRHD, palms out
7-8	Lock knees	Press DWN, palms DWN
1-8	RPT	

Transition to 4th POS L FWD

1-2	Rond de jambe R, 4th BK	Lift V POS OVRHD, palms up
3-4	Press R heel DWN	Press DWN, palms DWN
1-16	RPT plies 2 Xs, 4th BK	

Transition to 5th POS

1-2	Rond de jambe R 4th POS, R FWD	Lift V POS OVRHD
3-4	5th POS R FWD	Press DWN
1-2	Demi-plie	Lift 1st POS FWD
3-4	Grande plie	V POS OVRHD

ARMS V POSITION OVERHEAD, GRANDE PLIE

| 5-6 | Demi-plie | | Open 2nd POS C#1 (DIAG) |

DIAGONAL 2nd POSITION

| 7-8 | Lock knees | | DWN—L SHL C#2 |

5th POSITION,
ISOLATION SHOULDER

| 1-8 | RPT above 8 CTS |

Transition to 5th POS L FWD

| 1-2 | Passe R TO | | JH X OVRHD |

PASSE RIGHT, TURNED-OUT

| 3-4 | 5th POS R BK | | Press both DWN |
| 1-16 | RPT plies 2 Xs, 5th BK |

Transition to 5th POS R FWD

| 1-2 | Passe R TO | | JH X OVRHD |
| 3-4 | 5th POS R FWD | | DWN |

Contractions with Locked Knees

| 1 | CON pelvis, AST HD L | | DWN, palms BK |

PELVIS CONTRACTION

2 3	Drop torso DWN L		On FLR
4	HD to knee		
5-6	TBTP torso, R C#1		Sides of torso
7-8	Recover upright		DWN
1-8	RPT		

Transition to 5th POS L FWD

1-2	**Passe R TO**	**JH X OVRHD**
3-4	**5th POS L FWD**	**DWN**
1-16	**RPT contractions 2 Xs**	
1-2	**Passe R NTO**	**LJA 2nd**
3-4	**Plie L, DEV R FWD, flexed FT**	**JH 2nd**

DEVELOPE & ANKLE FLEX

5-6	**Grande rond de jambe 2nd PTD**	**R OVRHD, L 2nd**

GRANDE ROND DE JAMBE 2nd

7-8	**R arabesque**	
1	**R X BK L half toe**	**R FWD**

CROSS RIGHT BACK LEFT

2-4	**CON torso, REL C#1**	**R C#1**
1-12	**REV L**	
1-24	**RPT R-L**	

"People who never stand still are healthier for it."

Rib-Cage and Pelvis Isolations

FT 5th POS, R FWD, lock   Arms 1st POS

COUNTS	BODY MOVEMENT	ARMS
1	Plie L, AST tendu R FWD half toe TO, knee bent	LJA 2nd
2-6	ISOL RC R-L on beat	

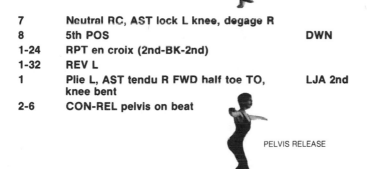

RIB-CAGE ISOLATION RIGHT

7	Neutral RC, AST lock L knee, degage R	
8	5th POS	DWN
1-24	RPT en croix (2nd-BK-2nd)	
1-32	REV L	
1	Plie L, AST tendu R FWD half toe TO, knee bent	LJA 2nd
2-6	CON-REL pelvis on beat	

PELVIS RELEASE

7	Neutral pelvis, AST lock L, degage R	
8	5th POS	
1-24	RPT en croix	DWN
1-32	REV L	
1	Plie L, AST tendu R FWD half toe TO, knee bent	LJA 2nd
2-3	ISOL RC R-L	
4	Neutral RC, AST CON pelvis	JH 2nd
5	Neutral RC and pelvis	LJA 2nd
6	REL torso and HD	

RELEASE TORSO & HEAD

7	Neutral torso, HD, AST lock L, degage R	
8	5th POS	
1-24	RPT en croix	
1-32	REV L	

Glissade with Battement

FT 5th POS, R FRT, lock   Arms 1st

COUNTS	BODY MOVEMENT	ARMS
1-2	Glissade FWD (R glides FWD, L closes BK)	LJA 2nd
3-4	REV BK	
5	Battement R FWD TO PTD, L locked	
6	Plie L, flex R knee and FT TO	JH 2nd

FLEX ANKLE AND KNEE

7	Lock L knee, AST DEV battement R PTD TO	
8	5th POS R FWD	DWN
1-2	Glissade R 2nd (close L 5th FRT)	LJA 2nd
3-4	REV L (close R FRT)	
5	Battement R 2nd PTD	
6	Plie L, AST flex R knee and FT TO	JH 2nd
7	Lock L, AST DEV battement R PTD TO	
8	5th POS R BK	DWN
1-2	Glissade R BK (close L 5th FRT)	LJA 2nd
3-4	REV L FWD	
5	Battement R BK PTD TO	
6	Plie L, AST flex R knee and FT TO	JH 2nd
7	Lock L knee, AST DEV battement BK, R PTD TO	LJA 2nd

BACK BATTEMENT

8	5th POS R BK	
1-8	RPT 2nd POS	
1-32	REV all L	

Developpe Stretch

Begin 1st POS NTO   Arms DWN

COUNTS	BODY MOVEMENT	ARMS
1-4	**Passe R NTO**	**LJA 2nd**
5-8	**Pulse knee upward**	**Both HNDS on knee**
1-4	**Developpe R FWD**	**Both HNDS on FT or ankle**

ANKLE HOLD FORWARD

5-8	**Pulse R upward**	**Same**
1-4	**Hold extension FWD**	**LJA 2nd**

HOLD EXTENSION

5-8	**Lower R FLR, PT, close 1st PP**	**DWN**
1-24	**REV L**	
1-4	**Passe R TO**	**LJA 2nd**
5-8	**Pulse knee upward**	**R HND on R knee, L 2nd**
1-4	**Stretch R 2nd**	**R HND on R FT, L 2nd**

ANKLE HOLD 2nd

5-8	**Pulse R upward**	**Same**
1-4	**Hold extension 2nd**	**LJA 2nd**
5-8	**Lower R FLR, PT, close 1st PP**	**DWN**
1-24	**REV L**	
1-4	**Passe R NTO**	**LJA 2nd**
5-8	**Passe R TO**	**R HND R knee, L 2nd**
1-4	**R attitude BK**	**Same**
5-8	**Pulse R upward**	**Same**

ATTITUDE KNEE HOLD

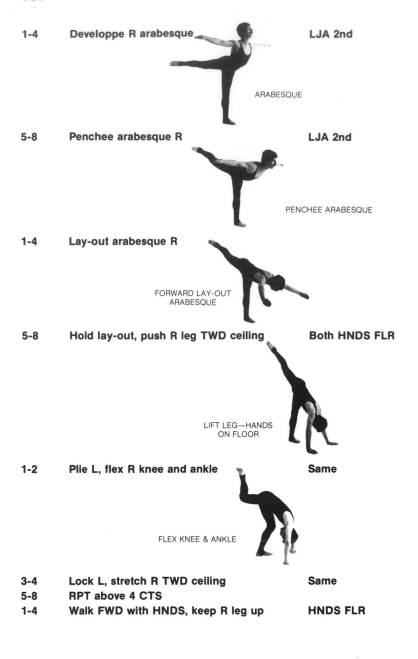

1-4	**Developpe R arabesque**	**LJA 2nd**

ARABESQUE

5-8	**Penchee arabesque R**	**LJA 2nd**

PENCHEE ARABESQUE

1-4	**Lay-out arabesque R**	

FORWARD LAY-OUT
ARABESQUE

5-8	**Hold lay-out, push R leg TWD ceiling**	**Both HNDS FLR**

LIFT LEG—HANDS
ON FLOOR

1-2	**Plie L, flex R knee and ankle**	**Same**

FLEX KNEE & ANKLE

3-4	**Lock L, stretch R TWD ceiling**	**Same**
5-8	**RPT above 4 CTS**	
1-4	**Walk FWD with HNDS, keep R leg up**	**HNDS FLR**

5-8	Slowly lower chest FLR	HNDS FLR

CHEST TO FLOOR—
HOLD ARABESQUE

1-4	Turn toes under, walk up to INV V POS	Same
5-8	Wrap arms around legs, HD to knees	

WRAP ARMS AROUND LEGS

1-8	Slowly uncurl to standing POS, CON	1st POS
1-64	REV above L (passe L NTO, L HND holds L knee)	

Center Adage

Begin 1st POS NTO, lock   Arms DWN

COUNTS	BODY MOVEMENT	ARMS
1-4	R passe NTO, DEV FWD	LJA, JH 2nd
5-6	Grande rond de jambe 2nd	R OVRHD, L 2nd
7-8	Grande rond de jambe arabesque	Same
1-4	Low passe R, lean TWD L hip	V POS OVRHD

PASSE & SIDE STRETCH

5	R X L AST CON torso	Slice R DWN

RIGHT CROSS LEFT & CONTRACT

6-8	Corkscrew turn L, end both FT 1st POS NTO	V POS OVRHD on 8
1-2	Grande plie, 1st POS NTO, AST CON torso	Pull elbows DWN

| 3-6 | Lay-out, arch BK | Both BK and OVRHD |

LAY-OUT BACK

7-8	Recover torso—upright	DWN
1-2	Lunge R FWD, TO	V POS OVRHD
3-4	Hold	Press R FWD, L 2nd

4th POSITION ARMS

5-8	Double inside turn R, ending 5th POS. Plie L FWD on 8, AST ISOL R SHL FWD on 8	Both chest for turn, LJA 2nd on 8
1-2	Lunge L FWD	LJA 2nd
3-6	Lay-out, arch BK	Elbows BK and OVRHD

LUNGE LAY-OUT

| 7-8 | Recover torso | V POS OVRHD |
| 1-3 | Pivot R, AST grande plie 2nd POS | Pull both X FRT body, open 2nd POS JH |

GRANDE PLIE 2nd

4	Lunge R upstage	R 2nd, L FWD
5-8	Double outside turn L, ending 5th POS. R plie, L half-toe, on 8, AST ISOL R SHL on 8	Both chest for turn, LJA 2nd on 8
1-24	REV above 24 CTS L	

1-2	R attitude BK, AST ISOL R SHL FWD	LJA 2nd

RIGHT ATTITUDE—
RIGHT SHOULDER ISOLATION

3-4	R attitude FWD, AST ISOL L SHL FWD	Same

RIGHT ATTITUDE—
LEFT SHOULDER ISOLATION

5-6	Developpe R C#1	Same
7-8	Lunge R C#1	Same
1-8	REV L	
1	R attitude BK, AST ISOL R SHL FWD	LJA 2nd
2	R attitude FWD, AST ISOL L SHL FWD	Same
3	Develope R C#1	Same
4	Lunge R C#1	Same
5-8	REV L	
1-2	Step BK R-L	DWN
3	Drag L cou de pied, AST ISOL RC. Lean TWD passe leg TO	4th high

SUR LE COU DE PIED

4	Step L	DWN
5-8	REV L	
1-8	RPT above 8 CTS	
1	Battement R 2nd POS TO	LJA 2nd
2	Hold battement, AST ISOL RC L	

BATTEMENT AND
RIB-CAGE ISOLATION

3	Releve L AST passe R TO, RC lift L, lean TWD R	4th high

PASSE TURNED-OUT

4	Step R	DWN
5-8	REV L	
1-2	Pique R, AST arabesque L and balance	R JH OVRHD, L behind waist
3-4	Plie R, AST cou de pied L, AST ISOL L SHL FWD	

ISOLATION LEFT SHOULDER

5-6	Pique L BK, R low battement FWD balance	L JH OVRHD, R JH 2nd
7-8	Plie L, cou de pied R, AST ISOL R SHL FWD	
1-2	Pique R 2nd, L low battement 2nd balance	R JH 2nd, L hip
3-4	Plie R, cou de pied L, AST ISOL L SHL FWD	
5-6	Pique L 2nd, R low battement 2nd balance	L JH 2nd, R hip
7-8	Plie L, cou de pied R, AST ISOL R SHL FWD	

ISOLATION RIGHT SHOULDER

1-16	RPT above 16 CTS	
1	Battement R BK PTD TO, L locked	4th opposition
2	Grande rond de jambe R 2nd POS TO PTD, L locked	LJA 2nd

"Muscles are beautiful."

| 3 | Plie L, hold 2nd battement, ISOL RC L, lean TWD R leg | 4th high, L up, R 2nd |

BATTEMENT

4	R X L	R slice, L DWN
5-6	Corkscrew turn L with contraction	DWN
7-8	Hip lift R, step R, C#1	4th opposition C#1
1-8	REV L	
1-16	RPT above 16 CTS except on CT 3 each time releve locked knee instead of plie	

RELEVE SUPPORTING LEG

| 1&2 | Triple BK R-L-R | DWN |
| 3 | L attitude 2nd TI, AST ISOL L SHL FWD | LJA 2nd |

ATTITUDE 2nd POSITION
TURNED-IN

| 4 | Battement L C#1 TO, AST ISOL R SHL FWD | |
| 5-8 | REV L (ISOL L SHL) | |

BATTEMENT 2nd—
ISOLATION LEFT SHOULDER

1-8	RPT	
1	Step R FWD	1st
2	Passe L NTO	LJA 2nd

3-4	Plie R, flex L knee and FT FWD, AST CON torso	JH 2nd
5-6	Releve R, developpe L, PTD TO, AST REL torso	V POS OVRHD, palms out
7-8	Lunge FWD L, NTO	DWN
1-8	REV L	
1-16	RPT above 16 CTS	
1	Step L FWD TO	DWN
2	Plie L TO, AST TENDU R 2nd POS, AST TBTP lay-out FWD	LJA 2nd

TENDU RIGHT 2nd—
TABLETOP LAY-OUT FORWARD

3-4	Hold above POS and lift R 2nd NTO	Same
5-8	Hold 2nd POS, lift torso L, end 2nd POS lay-out	
1-8	REV R	
1-16	RPT above 16 CTS, lunge L FWD last 8 CTS	

MULTIPLE CHAINES, HEAD ISOLATION AND LEAP—
Allegro—Center Progression, Across the Floor

FT 4th POS, R FRT on toe   Face S#6
Arms 4th, R FRT

COUNTS	BODY MOVEMENT	ARMS
1&2&3	2, R chaine turns ending with R FWD on 3	
4	Step L FWD (lunge)	V POS OVRHD
5	Step R FWD	Sundari HD R, HNDS at pelvis
6-7	REV & RPT (L and R)	Sundari HD L & R, HNDS at pelvis
&8	Catch step L-R BK, FRT, AST Sundari HD BK, FWD	2nd LJA
1	Step L FWD	1st
2	R FT FRT, 5th POS plie	
3	Jump with legs together 5th	2nd LJA
&	Open R leg FWD, L BK (in air)	
4	Land R leg plie with L in arabesque	OVRHD
5	Step L FWD	Sundari HD L, HNDS at hips
6-7	REV and RPT (R and L)	Sundari HD R, L, HNDS at pelvis
&8	Catch step R-L BK, FWD, AST Sundari HD BK, FWD	2nd LJA
1-16	RPT all above	Same

PREPARATION FOR
CHAINE TURNS

LUNGE FORWARD

SUNDARI HEAD RIGHT

CHAINE AND BATTEMENT COMBINATION—
Allegro—3/4 Center Progression, Travels S#8 and S#6

FT 1st POS, NTO, lock   Arms 1st

COUNTS	BODY MOVEMENT	ARMS
1	Pique R with L, low 2nd POS off FLR	R OVRHD, L 2nd
2	Step L X R plie, slight side stretch L	Pull R elbow DWN X chest and ISOL L SHL
3&4&	R chaine turns	Arms at chest
5	Step R in plie 2nd (to C#1)	X FRT of pelvis

6	Battement L across FRT of R to C#1	2nd POS ILJA
1-6	REV to L	
1-5	RPT the above R (Step R 2nd)	
6	Battement L 2nd	2nd POS, ILJA
1-6	REV	
1-5	RPT the above R (Step R 2nd)	
6	Arabesque L leg BK	V POS FRT of SHLS
1-6	REV L	
6, 6's	RPT all above	Same

The above is done with supporting foot flat,
in releve, and with saute. When done in 8's add two
chaine turns on 5&6&, step on 7, plie.

PIQUE RIGHT, LEFT 2nd   XROL—PULL ELBOW DOWN   BATTEMENT L X R

ISOLATION STUDY
—Center Progression

FT, R toe PT BK   Arms 1st

COUNTS	BODY MOVEMENT	ARMS
	I	
1	R SHL ISOL roll BK. AST step FWD R NTO, demi-plie	DWN

ROLL SHOULDER BACK

2	Step L FWD	L arms opens slightly 2nd
3	ISOL rib-cage R, AST step R	HNDS on pelvis

RIB-CAGE RIGHT

| 4 | Step L | Jazz wrist press R 2nd |
| 5-6 | Plie R TI 2nd POS (¼ turn L) | Same |

TURN-IN RIGHT, DEEP PLIE

| 7 | Step BK R, AST HD thrust FWD | HNDS on pelvis |
| 8 | Step BK L, AST HD thrust FWD | Same |

II

| 1 | R 2nd POS TI, plie (CON torso) | 2nd POS |

TURN-IN RIGHT, SECOND

2	Step L, AST CON and thrust L hip	Same
3	Step R, AST R SHL roll BK	DWN
4	Step L, AST L SHL thrust	
5	Step R 2nd POS	R palm up, bend from elbow

LIFT RIGHT HAND

6	Plie L, AST L rib cage ISOL	R arm 2nd POS
7	Hip lift R	R wrist circle at hip
8	Hip lift L	V POS OVRHD

III

| 1 | Step R FWD, NTO, plie | L JH OVRHD |
| 2 | Step L (same) | R FWD, bent at elbow, L parallel to torso bent at elbow, JH palms TWD body |

3-4	Step R-L, ISOL hip R 2 Xs	2nd POS
5	FT parallel, plie to FLR, face C#1	DWN

PLIE TO FLOOR

6	Stand and arch	V POS OVRHD

STAND AND ARCH

&7	Tap R, step R to C#1, AST CON and REL torso	2nd POS
&8	REV L	Same

IV

1-2	Step R-L, AST HD roll R	2nd
&3	Hip lift R FWD	R wrist at R hip
&4	Hip lift L to L	REV
5-6	Step R-L, AST ISOL HD R-L (Sundari)	
7	Step BK R	Jazz wrist press OVRHD—R arm

PRESS WRIST OVERHEAD

8	REV L	REV L (wrist press OVRHD)
1	Step R FWD	R arm 2nd POS
2	Step L FWD	REV L
&3	Lunge R X BK L	R arm scoops across body (palm up)

LUNGE RIGHT BACK—
SCOOP RIGHT ARM

&4	Lunge and step R FWD	R arm scoops FWD
5-8	REV L	
1-8	RPT above	
6,8's	RPT all above from beginning	Same

Cuban Square

FT 1st PP, NTO   Arms 1st

COUNTS	BODY MOVEMENT	ARMS
1	XROL plie	Arms cross low FRT of body
2	Step L 2nd, ISOL R hip	2nd LJA

RIGHT HIP ISOLATION

COUNTS	BODY MOVEMENT	ARMS
3	Step R BK, ISOL L hip	Hold
4	XLOR, hips FWD	Arms cross FRT
5	Step R 2nd, ISOL L hip	Open 2nd LJA
6	Step L BK, ISOL R hip	
7&8	Triple R, L, R, FWD	Jazz HNDS push FWD 2nd POS
1-8	REV and RPT	Same as above
1-16	RPT R and L above	
	Also done with funky up beat.	

Diagonal Hip Lift

COUNTS	BODY MOVEMENT	ARMS
&1	Hip lift R and step R C#1, FT parallel 2nd	4th POS, L FRT, R 2nd

HIP LIFT

COUNTS	BODY MOVEMENT	ARMS
2&3	Triple turning L, stepping L-R-L	DWN at sides
4	Step R to C#1, CON torso	L arm FWD leading with wrist
5-8	REV	
1-16	RPT R and L above	

Jazz Rock

1-2	Step FWD R, L, plie	R arm swings BK and 2nd, with BK of HND leading
3-4	Step R in place, L BK	FWD and pulls BK at elbow CT 4
5-6	Step R in place, L directly in FRT	R swings BK, 2nd, FWD
7&8	Triple R-L-R (step BK, BK, FRT)	R arm shoots OVRHD and DWN FWD
1-8	REV and RPT L	
1-8	RPT R using both arms in the port de bras	

BACK OF HANDS, 2nd

1-8	RPT L side with both arms
1-16	RPT R and L above

Also done with funky up beat.

Jazz Star

TAP AND CONTRACT

1-2	Tap R FRT, step R FWD, CON torso on CT1, release on CT 2	V POS FWD to 2nd LJA CT 2
3	XLOR	1st
4&5	Triple R-L-R traveling to R side	Arms swing up 2nd LJA
6-7	Tap L FRT, step L, CON and REL rib-cage	V POS FWD to 2nd on CT 7
8	Step R FWD	Push FWD jazz HNDS 2nd
1-8	RPT and REV above, tap L	
1-16	RPT R and L above	

Also done with funky up beat.

Oriental Walk Combination

ORIENTAL HAND PUSH DOWN

1-2	Walk FWD R plie, NTO	L arm pushes DWN FRT, flexed wrist
3-4	RPT L	REV
5-8	RPT above	L pushes OVRHD, flexed wrist, then R
1	Step R to 2nd	R arm OVRHD
2-3	Step BK L, step R in place	R HND in to SHL and push 2nd flexed wrist, L arm FWD CT 3
4	OTL plie	Into chest
5	Releve R with L neutral passe	OVRHD V POS
6	Step FWD L plie	
7	Step BK R	Arms DWN
8	Close L 1st POS, NTO, CON torso	1st
1-2	Step FWD R, L	Swing BK and FRT, leading with BK of wrists
3-4	Step R in place, cross L in BK	CTS 3,4 circle 2nd to SHLS, shoot OVRHD V POS
5-6	RPT 1,2 above	Same as above
7&8	Step R-L-R (BK, BK, FRT)	Same as above
1-8	RPT and REV above, step L FWD	Same
1-16	RPT R and L above	Same

"Dance is a language. The words are the steps; the sentences are the order in which a choreographer has combined them."

Jazz Adage

JAZZ ADAGE — SOUS-SUS, ARABESQUE, LUNGE

2nd POS TO   Arms 1st   Sustain lyrical quality for each movement

COUNTS	BODY MOVEMENT	ARMS
1-4	Grande plie 2nd POS TO	Circle OVRHD, end 2nd jazz HNDS

GRANDE PLIE—2nd

5-8	REL and CON pelvis (RPT)	2nd jazz HNDS
1-4	RPT, grande plie	Same
5-8	ISOL rib-cage, R-L-R-L, as you ascend, end with locked knees	2nd POS LJA
1-32	RPT as above, on ascend use ISOL SHL in place of rib-cage	Same (on SHL ISOL start L)

Sous-Sus (Continue)

& 1-4	Sous-Sus (5th POS REL R FRT)	V POS OVRHD, move jazz HNDS to high 1st on CTS 2,3,4

SOUS-SUS

5-8	CON rib-cage and swing HD L to R slowly—hold sous-sus POS	Hold Jazz HNDS (High 1st)
1-4	Grande plie 5th POS TO	Circle OVRHD, press to 2nd, and press to 1st
5-8	Ascend—press L SHL FWD and R SHL BK on a DIAG line	Hold 1st
1-8	Hold balance 5th POS REL (heel DWN CT 8)	Lift to V POS OVRHD
3, 8's	RPT & REV above, start with sous-sus, 5th L FRT	Same

Arabesque Promenade (Continue)

1-4	Heels to FLR	Press to 1st POS
5-8	Low arabesque L	Press to LJA 2nd

LOW ARABESQUE

1-16	Promenade (hold arabesque), lift heel of R and make quarter turn R.	Same
	1-4 Face S#8	
	5-8 Face S#7	
	1-4 Face S#6	
	5-8 Face FRT (S#5)	
1-16	RPT promenade arabesque L, add L arm circle. (Make quarter turn R as above)	L arm circles OVRHD, end 2nd ILJA
1-4	CON rib-cage and pelvis, plie R, passe L, NTO	2nd POS jazz HNDS
5-6	Lock R knee	2nd LJA
7-8	Developpe L FWD and step L 1st	1st POS
1-8	Releve 5th POS L FRT, lock knees	Lift to V POS OVRHD, slowly
1-8	Hold balance 5th (heels to FLR, 7-8)	Hold
6, 8's	RPT all above from arabesque promenade (arabesque R and promenade L)	

Lunge (Continue)

1-4	Lunge (deep) R to C#2 NTO	2nd LJA

DEEP LUNGE

5-8	Turn L in grande plie 2nd TO	2nd jazz HNDS
1-4	Turn torso to C#1 (R STR, L bends)	Place R palm on FLR, elbow locked
5-8	HD looks to C#2—hold POS	Circle L HND to SHL and push L palm to C#2, R palm FLR
1-4	Hold POS	Slowly place R elbow on FLR

5-8	Turn to S#8, crouch POS, knees together between arms	Palms on FLR
1-2	Extend L leg BK, flex toes on FLR, lock L knee (R retains bent knee)	Same
3-4	Return to 1st—remain in crouch	Same
5-6	Extend and lock R leg BK (L retains bent knee)	Same
7-8	Return R to 1st—remain in crouch	Same
1-4	Extend both legs BK and return	Same
5-8	RPT both legs	Same
1-8	From 1st POS, body roll and lift to standing POS (still facing S#8)	Arms PP pull DWN from elbows to V POS BK

END OF BODY ROLL

6, 8's	RPT and REV from lunge above (lunge L to C#1)	Same
1-16	Face FRT, FT 2nd NTO, bend from waist, let HD and SHL relax, take all tension from upper part of body.	Hang loose to FLR

LAY-OUT CENTER ADAGE

FT 1st PP, locked knees   Arms 1st

COUNTS	BODY MOVEMENT	ARMS

Lay-Out Back

LAY-OUT BACK

1-2	Passe neutral R	Lift 2nd POS LJA
3-4	Developpe R FWD	JH 2nd
5-6	Flex R FT	
7-8	Hold	Invert palms up
1-4	Lay-out BK (face looks at ceiling)	Same
5-8	Recover torso	
1-4	Passe neutral R	2nd

5-6	R DWN neutral 1st POS	DWN
7-8	Plie neutral and lock knees	2nd 7, DWN 8
1-24	REV all (use L leg)	

Lay-Out Side

LAY-OUT SIDE

1-2	Passe TO R leg	2nd LJA
3-4	Developpe R 2nd	
5-6	Flex R FT	
7-8	Hold	V POS OVRHD
1-4	Side lay-out to L	Same
5-8	Recover torso	Same
1-2	Passe to R (TO)	2nd LJA
3-4	Neutral passe R	
5-6	R DWN neutral 1st POS	DWN
7-8	Plie neutral and lock knees	2nd 7, DWN 8
1-24	REV & RPT (L and R)	
1-24	Lay-out can also be done FWD with leg 2nd	

Lay-Out Forward

LAY-OUT FORWARD—
LEG SECOND

1-2	Passe TO R	2nd LJA
3-4	Attitude BK	Same
5-6	Extend arabesque	Same
7-8	Flex FT	V POS OVRHD
1-4	FWD lay-out (arabesque)	Same

LAY-OUT FORWARD—
ARABESQUE

5-8	Recover arabesque	2nd POS LJA
1-2	Passe TO R	
3-4	Passe neutral R	
5-6	R DWN neutral 1st POS	DWN
7-8	Plie neutral and lock knees	2nd 7, DWN 8
1-24	REV all (use L leg)	

TRIPLES, SHOULDER ISOLATIONS AND
PORT DE BRAS—Across the Floor—Allegro

COUNTS	BODY MOVEMENT	ARMS
1&2	FWD triple R-L-R, NTO, ISOL L SHL 2	Lift 2nd POS

ISOLATION LEFT SHOULDER
—LONG JAZZ ARM

3&4	FWD triple L-R-L, ISOL R SHL 4	HNDS at chest

ISOLATION RIGHT SHOULDER
—CHEST

5&6	RPT R (ISOL L SHL)	BK of HNDS PP, reach to ceiling

ISOLATION LEFT SHOULDER
—ELBOWS DOWN

7&8	RPT L (ISOL R SHL)	Press DWN to 1st POS end in 1st POS

ISOLATION RIGHT SHOULDER
—LONG JAZZ ARM

1	XROL plie	DWN
2	Battement L, saute R, HD L	2nd POS, palms up
3&4	Triple L-R-L	DWN
5-6	Step R battement L, saute R, HD L	2nd POS, palms up
7&8	Triple L-R-L, face C#2	

1	Pique R FWD C#1	4th (R FRT)
2	Attitude L FWD, while on half toe R	4th (L FRT)

RELEVE—FORWARD ATTITUDE

3	Plie R, attitude L BK, AST pivot L to face C#2 (lay-out attitude, face FLR)	L FWD, R 2nd
4	Flex supporting leg in above POS	
5&6	Inside turn step L-R-L to C#2	
7-8	R leg swing FWD-BK to C#2	2nd LJA
1	Step R FWD C#1	Opposition
2	Lay-out attitude TO with flexed supporting leg	L FWD, R 2nd

LAY-OUT FORWARD—ATTITUDE

3	Plie R, stay in lay-out	R arm DWN TWD FLR
4	Flex R, still in lay-out	L FWD, R 2nd
5&6	Step L X BK R, step R 2nd, L 2nd	R 2nd, L circles 2nd
7	Tap R BK L, spiral torso, face BK	2nd, palms up
8	Spiral torso S#8, profile	Push palms S#8
4-8's	REV and RPT all above—triple L, R, L	

PLIE HOLDING FOOT ATTITUDE
—Adage

COUNTS	BODY MOVEMENT	ARMS
1-2	XROL, rond de jambe R to BK attitude	R arm across body, open 2nd
3-4	Hold R FT with L HND	R C#1
5-8	Plie in above POS and lock knee on 7, 8	
1-4	RPT plie	
5-8	RPT plie	
1-4	Developpe R C#1, Diagonal side lay-out C#2	2nd POS LJA (L HND to FLR, R OVRHD)
5-8	XROL turn L plie (corkscrew turn), end facing FRT	

1-4	Body roll, FT parallel 1st	DWN, BK, OVRHD V POS
5-8	Hold	Press DWN to 1st
4, 8's	RPT and REV all above (XLOR)	Same

The above is also done with pique
arabesque to C#1 as preparation 1-2
(L HND holds L FT, attitude)

HOLD RIGHT FOOT—ATTITUDE

JAZZ ADAGE—TORSO SPIRALS

FT—R BK 4th POS, PT toe, lunge FWD L
Arms 2nd LJA

COUNTS	BODY MOVEMENT	ARMS
1-2 (Slow)	Lunge R FWD, NTO—torso TBTP FWD, L lock, flex ankle	Spiral arms and rib-cage R to L (V POS OVRHD)

TORSO TABLETOP—SPIRAL
RIB-CAGE AND ARMS
RIGHT TO LEFT

3-4	Lunge L FWD, NTO—torso lay-out BK, spiraling R to L	Spiral arms and rib-cage R to L (V POS OVRHD, BK BD)

BEGINNING OF BACK LAY-OUT
SPIRAL RIB-CAGE AND ARMS
RIGHT TO CENTER

5-6	Lunge R to 2nd (grande plie), torso TBTP FWD	Spiral arms and rib-cage R to L
&7,8	Hold 2nd, lock knees, torso lay-out BK, spiraling R to CTR (BK lay-out is on CT 7—lunge R BK). Square POS on CT 8, close R to L.	Spiral arms and rib-cage R to CTR—2nd ILJA on CT 7, LJA 2nd CT 8

END OF LAY-OUT,
SPIRAL BACK

1-8	RPT and REV L (lunge L FWD)	Same—spiral L to R
1-16	RPT all above R and L	Same
1-2	Lunge fall FWD to R FT, NTO, face S#8	Palms on FLR, below SHLS
3-4	Torso turns to face S#5, FT sous-sus POS (R BK)	L palm on FLR (elbow lock), R OVRHD, LJA

SOUS-SUS WITH
LEFT PALM ON FLOOR

| 5-6 | Lunge R FWD, TBTP, S#8 | V POS BK of SHLS |

LUNGE FORWARD—
ARMS V POSITION BACK

7&	Standing, FT 5th, R FRT, plie, TO, torso side stretch R (face S#5)	Bending to R side, V POS OVRHD
8	STR to square—hold 5th	L arm drops X torso to 1st, R arm 1st
1-8	REV and RPT lunge fall L	Same
1-16	RPT all above R and L	Same

JAZZ ADAGE—LYRIC STYLE—3/4 RHYTHM

FT—PT R FWD to C#2   Arms DIAG L FWD to C#2,
R BK to C#4

| COUNTS | BODY MOVEMENT | ARMS |

Phrase I

1-0 (slow)	Step R, L, 2nd, releve	Interlace fingers, push palms OVRHD
1-6	Step BK R plie, rond de jambe L (circle toe on FLR), sous-sus CTS 5-6, L FT BK	2nd LJA, CTS 1-4, V POS OVRHD CTS 5-6
1-6	REV 1-6 above, rond de jambe R, etc.	Same
1-6	Step R, L, 2nd, releve	Interlace fingers, push palms OVRHD
1-3	Step R 2nd, XLOR, step R 2nd	ISOL R SHL up and lift R arm
4-6	RPT and REV to L	ISOL L SHL up
1-6	RPT R and L above	Same

Phrase II

| 1-3 | PDB turn R (end 4th POS R FRT) | R HND pushes BK in 2nd, L on pelvis |
| 4-6 | Double outside turn L | Chest |

1-6	REV PDB turn L, OTR	Same
1-12	RPT R and L above	Same
1-3	Step FWD R plie, ITR lock, L FRT attitude	2nd LJA
4-6	Lunge L to C#1, XRBL	Reach R jazz HND to C#1, L on pelvis
1-6	REV and RPT above L (step L, ITL)	Same
1-12	RPT R and L above	Same

Phrase III

1-3	Step BK R, plie, L at neutral passe	Into waist, fists
4-6	High developpe L, R is in "plie-releve" POS	Pull elbows BK
& 1-6	Pivot to C#2 on "&" CT and REV, step BK L, etc.	Same
& 1-12	RPT R, L, above	Same
1-3	Step R FWD, plie, ITR, L BK attitude	V POS OVRHD
4-6	Hold plie—attitude POS, torso bends to L	Same
1-6	REV and RPT above	Same
1-12	RPT R, L above	Same
1-3	Pull R leg into neutral passe, facing FRT, lock L leg	2nd LJA
4-6	Descend to FLR on L leg, end in crouch POS on FLR	Descend to 1st

---

ADAGE—RENVERSE AND JAZZ SPLIT, SEAT-SPIN, 4/4 RHYTHM

FT—R FT crossed BK of L (deep lunge)
ISOL L SHL   Arms: R 2nd LJA, L on pelvis

COUNTS	BODY MOVEMENT	ARMS
1-8	Hold above POS	As above

Phrase I

1-2	Step RXL, plie, step L in place, renverse	DIAG, R DWN, L up
3-4	Releve L, R moves thru 2nd and to BK attitude TO (turn to R)	R jazz HND OVRHD, L 2nd
5-8	Extend R leg to FLR and into jazz split (R locks, L bends BK, TO)	R palm to FLR, L OVRHD (R palm touches FLR before L knee)
1-4	Knees into chest, seat-spin around R	L arm whips R, bring both arms into chest
5-8	End swastika POS (L bends FRT, R bends BK, both on FLR)	2nd LJA
1-4	Lift to kneeling POS on both knees, 2nd POS	1st at sides

5-8	Hold kneeling POS	Lift arms to 2nd, LJA
1-4	Drop torso BK to knee hinge, with SHLS on FLR	2nd, palms on FLR
5-6	Lift torso to kneeling POS	R OVRHD, L FWD of chest
7-8	Step L, R, FWD—stand	1st POS

Phrase II

1-2	Step L FWD, ISOL R knee TI	2nd jazz HNDS
3-8	Torso spirals FWD, L side and to BK lay-out — ISOL L SHL	L arm 2nd, R circles FWD, to L side, OVRHD and 2nd
1-4	Lunge to L, and turn torso L and end facing BK — R is stretched to side	2nd ILJA
5&6	1½ OTR (end facing FRT), R leg at passe, NTO	Into chest
7-8	Step R BK, plie, CT 7, releve R, passe L TO — arch BK, CT 8	R OVRHD, L 2nd
1-2	Hold arch POS	Hold
3-4	Face FRT, plie L, releve L — R holds TO passe	Circle OVRHD and 2nd LJA
5-6	RPT plie, releve, CTS 3-4 above	Same
7&8	Step FWD, R, L, PT R 2nd, plie	X FRT chest, end R FWD, L BK OVRHD
3, 8's	REV and RPT all of Phrase II above (start R FWD and TI L)	RPT

A CHOREOGRAPHED MODERN JAZZ CENTER BARRE II

For building flexibility, strength and endurance.
Music for 4/4—Slow, lyric jazz music

| COUNTS | BODY MOVEMENT | ARMS |

Introduction

| 1-8 | Hold—R toe BK | |

HOLD INTRODUCTION

1-8	Hold	Arms slowly lift to 2nd LJA
1-4	Step R FWD, develope L FRT, R "plie-releve" POS CT 3—Hold CT 4	Same
5-8	REV	
1-8	RPT above, R, L	

1st Phrase—Head Isolations

1-8	FT 1st NTO, circle HD R (slowly)	1st
1-8	Circle HD L	
1-8	Thrust HD FWD and BK (4 Xs)	
1-8	Move HD R, L (4 Xs)	
1-8	HD square (FWD, R side, BK, L side), RPT	
1-16	HD swings (L to R) (8 Xs)	
1-8	HD circle R	
1-8	HD circle L	
1-4	Step R FWD lunge (plie-releve POS)	4th POS, L FRT
5-6	Hold	ISOL L SHL FWD

ISOLATION LEFT SHOULDER FORWARD

7-8	Close R to L, plie 1st POS NTO on CT 7	1st POS CT 8
1-4	Hold plie, stretch torso to R	R lifts to 2nd
5-8	Hold	L lifts OVRHD
1-4	Walk FWD R-L-R-L	Spiral circle arms and torso (FWD, L, BK, R), V POS OVRHD

SPIRAL CIRCLE

5-8	Walk BK R-L-R-L	REV torso and arm circle

2nd Phrase—Chaines, Body Roll, Jazz Split

1-8	REV and lunge FWD L	Same as above
1-8	Stretch L as above	Same
1-8	Walk BK on beat, start R	1-2 LJA
		3-4 jazz HND 2nd
		5-6 Chest (BK of HND FRT)
		7-8 LJA and press DWN
1-8	Walk FWD, start R	RPT as above
1-4	Multiple chaine turns R (4 turns)	Into chest
5	1st POS plie, NTO (preparation)	1st

6	Stag leap to S#8, torso PP to FLR (R bends FWD, L BK attitude)	4th POS, L FWD
7-8	Land R, hold BK attitude, twist torso to C#2	Lift L arm OVRHD, look C#2 under L arm

TORSO TWIST—
BACK ATTITUDE

1-8	REV chaines and stag leap L	Same
1-2	Face C#2 and travel to C#4, step BK R and close L 1st releve NTO	V POS OVRHD
3-4	Grande plie	PP pull DWN with elbows

PARALLEL PULL DOWN—
ELBOWS

5-8	Body roll (push pelvis FWD and DK bend as knees straighten)	Carry BK to V POS
1-16	RPT body roll 2 Xs	
1-2	Step R over L, step L in place	R across FRT of body, L BK
3-4	Renverse turn R on L with R BK attitude	R OVRHD jazz HND, L 2nd

RENVERSE TURN WITH ATTITUDE

5-8	Slide into jazz split (R leg C#1)	L high, R on FLR
1-4	Seat-spin R (knees into chest)	Wrap around knees
5-8	Stand by tucking L under R, straighten R (face FRT)	LJA
1-2	Step BK L, close R 1st NTO	Cross arms FRT of pelvis, clenched fists
3-4	Hold plie	Explode jazz HNDS 2nd
5-8	RPT 4 CTS above	Same
1-4	RPT renverse turn, end C#2	
5-8	Step R plie C#2, L arabesque	V POS BK
1-4	Step BK L, close R 1st NTO (as above)	X arms and explode HNDS
5-8	RPT step BK L, R	RPT X and explode

3rd Phrase—Knee Hinges

1-4	Face C#1, step R 2nd POS NTO, releve both FT	V POS OVRHD
5-8	Hold releve, bend FWD (TBTP), torso PP to FLR	Same

TABLETOP BEND FORWARD

1-4	Drop to FLR, knee hinge	Cross FRT and open 2nd
5-8	Lie BK SHLS on FLR	2nd, palms on FLR
1-4	BK bend—arch and lift torso	V POS BK
5-6	Tuck toes under, CON and come to STR knees, torso PP to FLR, FT flat	Into SHLS and shoot OVRHD V POS
7-8	Straighten body	Press to 1st POS
1-8	Face C#2, RPT releve 2nd and TBTP	V POS OVRHD
1-4	Knee hinge, knees off FLR, heels up	Cross FRT and open 2nd
5-8	Hold hinge (45°)	ISOL L SHL FWD 5-6, LJA ISOL R SHL FWD 7-8, LJA

KNEE HINGE AND
SHOULDER ISOLATION

1-8	Step BK R, L releve 1st NTO (still face C#2) — Grande plie CTS 3-4, body roll CTS 5-8	V POS OVRHD, PP pull DWN, end V POS BK
1-4	Change direction to C#1, extend R toes to C#1 (locked knee), plie L and BK bend	Palms push to ceiling
5-8	Hold BK bend	Open 2nd LIJA
1-8	Straighten and swing R BK to deep lunge NTO	V POS OVRHD
1-8	Walk R-L (8 steps) and R to C#3	CT 1—R LJA CT 2—L LJA CT 3—R ILJA CT 4—L ILJA CT 5—swing R OVRHD CT 6—swing L OVRHD CT&7—Both circle FRT of chest —end 2nd LJA CT 8—press to 1st 1st POS
1-8	Face C#3, step R 2nd NTO, grande plie (release HD and pelvis, exhale) 5-8 CON (inhale) lift to upright POS	

4th Phrase—Progressive Developpes

1-4	Developpe R TO FWD (waist height) C#3	2nd jazz HNDS

DEVELOPPE RIGHT FORWARD

5-8	Demi-plie L, lifting R higher	Same
1-4	Rond de jambe R to 2nd—lock L	V POS OVRHD
5-8	Demi-plie L, lifting R higher	Same
1-4	Rond de jambe R to arabesque—lock L	4th POS, R FWD
5-8	Demi-plie, lifting R	Same

DEMI-PLIE IN ARABESQUE

1-4	Turn body to C#2, side lay out L, lock R	V POS OVRHD
5-8	Demi-plie L, lifting R (lock L on CT 8)	Same
1	Fouette R FWD 4th POS, face C#1	2nd LJA
2-3	Plie, releve L, BK lay-out, lifting R leg higher	Same

BACK LAY-OUT

4	Step R C#1	1st
5&6	Run L, R, L to C#1	1st
7-8	Releve 4th POS NTO—plie CT 8	V POS OVRHD CT 7, 2nd POS jazz HNDS CT 8
1-40	RPT and REV all of above Phrase 4. Face C#1 (end facing FRT on CTS 39-40, releve and plie)	
1-8	Brush R leg, FRT, BK (8 Xs), L locked	ILJA
1-4	Step BK R, close L 1st NTO	Cross arms FRT of pelvis, fists, and explode jazz HNDS 2nd, hold CT 4
5-8	RPT above	Same
1-8	Brush L leg, FRT, BK (8 Xs), R locked	ILJA

1-8	Developpe R FWD TO to arabesque penchee	2nd POS LJA

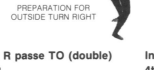

ARABESQUE PENCHEE

1-8	Step BK R-L (gradual demi-plie CTS 3-8), CON on CTS 7-8 (1st POS)	Push from SHLS OVRHD, press to 2nd to 1st
1-8	RPT 8 CTS above	

5th Phrase—Turns

1-4	Walk BK R-L-R, step L FWD, plie 4th	4th POS, R FRT prep for turn

PREPARATION FOR
OUTSIDE TURN RIGHT

5-8	OTR releve L with R passe TO (double)	Into chest
1	Step R tombe C#2	4th POS, R FRT
2-4	ITR releve R with L passe TO (double)	Into chest
5-8	Step L plie FRT of R 5th, sous-sus (hold 6, 7, 8)	1st jazz HNDS
1-4	Demi-plie 5th on releve	2nd jazz HNDS

DEMI-PLIE 5th

5-8	Lock knees	Same
1-4	Step BK, L-R-L, step R FWD (4th POS)	4th POS L FRT (prep for turn)
5-8	OTL on releve R with L passe TO (double)	Into chest
1	Step L tombe C#2	4th POS, L FRT
2-4	ITL on releve L with R passe TO	Into chest
5-8	Step R, plie FRT of L 5th, sous-sus (hold 6, 7, 8)	1st jazz HNDS
1-4	Demi-plie 5th on releve	2nd jazz HNDS
5-8	Lock knees	Same
1	Step R 2nd (face FRT)	R rounded OVRHD
2	XLOR	R crosses FRT of chest

| 3-4 | Step R 2nd, tap plie L BK to 4th | R to 2nd jazz HND, ISOL L SHL |

ISOLATION LEFT SHOULDER

5-8	RPT and REV above L	Same
1-2	Step R 2nd (face FRT) plie, L at pique POS FRT TO, releve R CT 2	R rounded OVRHD, L 1st
3-4	REV	
5-8	RPT R and L	
1	Step BK R plie	Fist X FRT of chest
2-3	Step L 2nd plie, step R FWD plie	2nd POS jazz HNDS
4	Battement L FWD, flex ankle, R plie	2nd jazz HND
5-8	REV	
1-8	RPT above 8 CTS	Same
1-2	Step R 2nd, XLOR	R OVRHD, L 2nd, pull R elbow to chest CT 2
3-6	Multiple chaine turns R (4 turns)	Into chest
7	Step R 2nd	V POS OVRHD, palms out
8	Tap L BK to 4th	Press to 2nd, ISOL L SHL
1-8	REV L	Same
1-16	RPT above R and L, travel to S#7, and FRT to S#5	Same
1-16	Step R, L to C#1 Deep lunge on L, R BK, slowly lift R leg in attitude NTO keep L in plie, torso PP to FLR. Slowly twist upper torso to C#2. HD looks to C#2.	Start 2nd, slowly move OVRHD and open 2nd

TORSO TWIST—ATTITUDE

| 1-16 | Step R 2nd, L BK 4th, low bow (8 CTS) Reverse bow L | R circles 2nd OVRHD, 2nd L circles |

"Get yourself moving."

OUTSIDE TURNS RIGHT AND LEFT

5th POS TO, R FT FRT   Arms 1st
(If turning R, turn on L FT or vice-versa)

COUNTS	BODY MOVEMENT	ARMS
1-2	PT R toes 2nd, L locks in place	2nd POS LJA

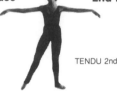

TENDU 2nd

COUNTS	BODY MOVEMENT	ARMS
3-4	Step R BK 4th POS TO	4th POS, R FRT, L 2nd
5&6&	Double OTR, R at passe NTO, L demi-plie, snap HD on "&" CTS	Into chest
7-8	Close R demi-plie 5th, BK of L	2nd ILJA, ISOL L SHL FWD
1-8	RPT and REV all above L (PT L toes 2nd)	Same
	Triple turns—done same as above. Snap HD on 5&6&7&, ISOL on CT 8.	

INSIDE TURNS RIGHT AND LEFT

1st POS NTO   Demi-plie   Arms 1st
(If turning R, turn on R FT or vice-versa)

COUNTS	BODY MOVEMENT	ARMS
1&2	Triple FWD, R-L-R, NTO, demi-plie	4th POS R FRT, L 2nd
3&4&	Double ITR, L at passe NTO, R demi-plie, snap HD on "&" CTS	Into chest

NEUTRAL PASSE

COUNTS	BODY MOVEMENT	ARMS
5-8	RPT and REV above L (triple L-R-L)	Same
	Triple turns done as above. Snap HD on 3&4&5&, triple BK L-R-L on 7&8. Close R to L NTO, locked knees CT 8.	

MULTIPLE CHAINE (2 step) TURNS

Torso faces S#6   PT R toe FWD
Stand on locked L   Arms 4th, R FWD
Done traveling across FLR

PREPARATION FOR CHAINE TURN

COUNTS	BODY MOVEMENT	ARMS
1&	Step R (turn R), step L to complete turn —HD snaps on "&" CTS	Into chest
1-16	Turns are done 16 CTS across FLR Turns may be done in releve, demi-plie, or grande plie	
1-16	RPT and REV, turning L	Same

ATTITUDE TURNS

4th POS, R BK, L FRT   Arms 2nd LJA
Done traveling across FLR

COUNTS	BODY MOVEMENT	ARMS
1	Step R FWD, demi-plie	2nd POS LJA
2	ITR, turn R on R, releve, L FRT attitude TO	2nd POS LJA

FRONT ATTITUDE TURN RIGHT

3	Step L FWD, demi-plie, R FT BK	Same
4	Releve L (turn R), R leg BK, attitude TO	4th POS, R jazz HND OVRHD, L 2nd LJA
1-12	Continue series of turns across FLR	

ATTITUDE TURN AND HIP LIFT

4th POS, R BK, L FRT   Arms 2nd LJA

COUNTS	BODY MOVEMENT	ARMS
1	Step R FWD demi-plie	2nd POS LJA
2	ITR, turn on R releve, L FRT attitude TO	2nd POS LJA
3	Face FRT, passe L, NTO, plie	Cross wrists FRT of chest

&4	High hip lift L, releve R, & step L	4th POS, R FRT, L 2nd

HIGH HIP LIFT

5-6	Step BK, plie, NTO, R-L	1st
7&8&	Step FWD R plie (prep for ITR), double turn R-L at passe neutral. Snap HD on "&" CTS.	4th POS, R FRT, L 2nd, move into chest
1-8	RPT and REV (step L FWD plie)	Same
1-16	RPT R and L above	

OUTSIDE AND LEAP TURN COMBINATION

PP 1st POS, locked knees   Arms 1st

COUNTS	BODY MOVEMENT	ARMS
1&2	Triple FWD plie R-L-R (torso twist)	Move from 1st to 4th POS, L arm FRT

TORSO TWIST

3&4&	Double OTL on R plie, L passe NTO	Into chest
5-6	Releve R, developpe L FRT CT 5, step L FWD plie	2nd LJA
7&8&	Leap turn R (chaine FWD R plie, step R-L on CTS 7&, jete R FWD CT 8), double ITR on R plie, L at passe NTO	Into chest, open 2nd on jete, return to chest for ITR
1-8	RPT and REV above triple L-R-L	
1-16	RPT R and L above	Same

ATTITUDE TURN AND DEVELOPPE

4th POS, R BK, L FRT   Arms 2nd LJA

COUNTS	BODY MOVEMENT	ARMS
1	Step R FWD demi-plie	2nd POS LJA
2	ITR on R releve, L BK attitude TO	2nd pushing BK from SHLS, flex wrists

BACK ATTITUDE TURN RIGHT

3	Passe L BK of R TO, R demi-plie	Cross arms FRT of chest
4	Developpe L 2nd releve R, torso leans R	Arms DIAG R DWN, L up
5-8	RPT and REV above step L, FWD plie	Same
1-8	RPT R and L above	Same

RENVERSE AND CHAINE COMBINATION

Lunge L to C#1, R crossed BK 4th
Arms LJA 2nd

COUNTS	BODY MOVEMENT	ARMS
1	XROL plie, L in place	DIAG—R DWN, L up

DIAGONAL ARMS

2&	Releve L, rond de jambe R 2nd to BK attitude TO	2nd LJA
3	OTR, L locked, R BK attitude, arch BK	2nd press BK from SHLS
4	Plie L, developpe R, FRT TO	Palms push FRT from SHLS
5&6	Triple R-L-R FWD, NTO, plie	Circle DWN, end 2nd palms BK
7&8&	Multiple chaine turns L, step L-R-L-R, demi-plie	Into chest
1-8	RPT and REV above XLOR	Same
1-16	RPT R and L above	Same

CHAINE JETE AND CHAINE LEAP TURN

Torso faces S#6   PT R toe FWD   Stand on locked L
Arms 4th, R FWD   Done traveling across FLR

PREPARATION FOR TURN

COUNTS	BODY MOVEMENT	ARMS
1-2	Chaine turn R (step R, L, demi-plie)	Into chest
&3	Jete R FRT, L BK attitude TO	4th L OVRHD, R 2nd
4	Step L FWD 4th, plie	High 1st jazz HNDS
5-8	RPT above	Same
1-8	RPT above adding ITR plie on CTS "&4" —L at passe NTO. Step L on CT 4, RPT 5,8.	Same
1-8	RPT chaine leap turns across FLR	Same

LEAP TURN AND MULTIPLE CHAINE TURNS

Torso faces S#6   PT R toes FWD   Stand on locked L
Arms 4th, R FWD, L 2nd   Done making circle R

COUNTS	BODY MOVEMENT	ARMS
1-2	Chaine turn R (step R-L, demi-plie)	Into chest
&3	Jete R FRT, L BK attitude TO	4th, L OVRHD, R 2nd
&4	Land R and ITR plie, L at passe NTO step L on CT 4	Into chest
5-8	RPT above	
1-8	RPT 2 more Xs (this should complete circle R)	
1&2& to 6&	Multiple chaine turns R releve, travel on DIAG to C#1	Into chest
7-8	Step R FWD, plie on CT 7 (C#1) (Plie will help you stop after the momentum of multiple turns) — step L FWD, locked knee, CT 8	2nd POS LJA V POS OVRHD
1-4	Hold POS	Same

MULTIPLE INSIDE TURNS AND DEVELOPPE FRONT

Face C#2, lunge R FWD ½ toe, stretch L BK
Arms 4th, L FWD, R 2nd (palms out)

COUNTS	BODY MOVEMENT	ARMS
1-4	Run R-L-R-L to C#1	Move from 1st to V POS FRT

V POSITION OVERHEAD

5&6&	Multiple ITR, plie, L at passe NTO	Into chest
7	Releve R, developpe L FWD	2nd POS LJA
8	"Plie-releve" POS R leg, BK lay-out	Arms move to V POS BK
1-8	RPT and REV to C#2	Same
1-16	RPT all above	Same

"Keep at it."

CORKSCREW TURN (Spiral)

FT 1st PP POS
CON torso and HD   Arms 1st

COUNTS	BODY MOVEMENT	
1-2	Walk FWD plie PP, step R-L	1st POS
3-4	Step R 2nd PP, locked knee, CT 3, XLOR plie CT 4	Swing R 2nd LJA CT 3, circle L in OVRHD and out to 2nd

XROL PLIE

5-6	Releve turn R, end in plie with legs crossed. R is now FRT.	2nd POS LJA
7-8	Step BK L, R plie	1st POS
1-8	RPT and REV above walk plie L-R	Same
1-16	RPT R and L above	Same
	Also may be done adding OTL on CTS &7, lifting torso as you turn and step L-R on CTS &8	

MULTIPLE CHAINES IN A SQUARE—STOMP

LUNGE—
JAZZ HANDS 2nd

CT as if in 3/4 time against a 4/4 rhythm
Face S#6, lunge L FWD, R BK, locked knee
Arms 2nd jazz HNDS

ARMS

COUNTS	BODY MOVEMENT	
1&2&3	Chaine to S#5, step R-L-R-L CT 3 stomp R FWD 4th plie PP (to S#5)	Into chest Thrust high 1st jazz HNDS
4&5&6	Change direction spot S#8 — chaine — step R-L-R-L CT 6 stomp R FWD 4th plie PP (to S#8)	Same as above
7&8&1	Change direction spot S#7 — chaine — step R-L-R-L CT 1 stomp R FWD 4th plie PP (to S#7)	Same
2&3&4	Change direction spot S#6 Chaine — step R-L-R-L CT 4 stomp R FWD 4th plie PP (to S#6). (You have now completed the R square)	Same as above
1-8	Turn R and lunge R FWD, L BK (You are now ready to chaine L and complete an L square)	2nd POS jazz HNDS
1-12	RPT and REV above chaine L	Same
1-32	RPT R and L	Same

OUTSIDE TURN WITH BATTEMENT

FT 1st, PP, locked knees   Arms 1st

COUNTS	BODY MOVEMENT	ARMS
1-2	Step R, L FWD, plie, NTO	4th POS, R FRT, L 2nd

PREPARATION FOR
OUTSIDE TURN RIGHT

COUNTS	BODY MOVEMENT	ARMS
3-4	Single OTR and extend R Battement FWD, plie 3, releve 4	Cross chest CT 3, 2nd LJA CT 4
5-6	RPT turn and battement	Same

BATTEMENT RIGHT FORWARD

COUNTS	BODY MOVEMENT	ARMS
7&8	Triple FWD, R-L-R, "plie-releve" POS	2nd POS jazz HNDS
1-8	REV and RPT above L	Same
1-16	RPT R and L above	Same

JETE, CONTRACTION, CHAINE COMBINATION

FT 1st PP, locked knees   Arms 1st

COUNTS	BODY MOVEMENT	ARMS
1-2	Run R, L, plie	Lift to 2nd LJA
&3	Jete R	4th—L FWD, R 2nd
4	Passe L, NTO, CON torso	2nd jazz HNDS

PASSE LEFT—
CONTRACT TORSO

COUNTS	BODY MOVEMENT	ARMS
5&6&	Two chaine turns L, releve (Step L-R-L-R)	Chest
7&8	Step L plie CT 7, jete R CTS &8	Arms 1st CT 7, 4th POS L FRT
1-8	REV and RPT — start L (continue making large circle R)	Same
1-16	RPT R and L above — continue circle	

OUTSIDE TURN AND ARABESQUE

FT 1st PP, locked knees   Arms 1st

COUNTS	BODY MOVEMENT	ARMS
1-2	Step R, L FWD, plie, NTO	4th POS—R FRT, L 2nd
3	Single OTR, plie—R passe NTO	Chest
&4	Arabesque R, L plie	LJA 2nd

OUTSIDE TURN RIGHT
AND ARABESQUE RIGHT

5-6	Step R, L FWD, plie, NTO	4th POS—R FRT, L 2nd
7	Single OTR, plie—R passe NTO	Chest
&8	Arabesque R, L plie	LJA 2nd
1-2	Step R, L FWD, plie, NTO	4th POS—R FRT, L 2nd
3	Single OTR, plie—R passe NTO	Chest
&4	Passe R and developpe R 2nd, L plie &, releve CT 4	V POS OVRHD

DEVELOPPE RIGHT 2nd

5-6	Step R, L BK, plie, NTO	1st
7&8	Step R, L BK, releve, step R FWD, plie	Pull elbows BK at waist, push BK of HNDS FWD 2nd

BACK OF HANDS
FORWARD 2nd

1-16	REV and RPT above to L	Same
1-8	4 R turns with R leg 2nd (plie CT 1, releve 2, RPT)	2nd POS ILJA
1-4	Pull R leg into passe POS, plie, NTO, complete multiple OTR (2, 3 or 4)	Chest
5,6,7	Pose—R FT BK (deep lunge)	2nd POS, jazz HNDS

POSE   DEEP LUNGE

&8	Step R FWD, tap L BK of R	1st
1-16	REV and RPT turns in 2nd L	Same

ARABESQUE BARREL TURN

FT 1st PP, NTO, locked knees   Arms 1st

COUNTS	BODY MOVEMENT	ARMS
1-2	Step R, L FWD, plie, NTO	4th POS—R FRT, L 2nd
3&4	Double OTR, R at passe NTO, plie, extend R BK to arabesque	Chest—LJA on arabesque
5&6	RPT OTR and arabesque	Same
7&8	Barrel turn R, releve, R at passe NTO (HD spots FRT), step R FWD, plie on CT 8	DIAG POS FLR to ceiling (L DWN, then R DWN) 1st
1-8	REV and RPT above L	Same
1-16	RPT R and L	Same

PREPARATION FOR
BARREL TURN RIGHT

JAZZ COMBINATIONS

4/4—Moderate/fast musical percussion

COUNTS	BODY MOVEMENT	ARMS
1-8	Hold 4th POS, L FT BK (deep lunge)	2nd POS jazz HND

Phrase I   (ARABIAN)

1-2	Walk FWD L, R	Arms at sides
3	Jump to 2nd POS plie	Arms at sides
4	Hold plie on L FT, R heel TO passe with FT flexed, R knee TO	L arm OVRHD with bent elbow and jazz HND
5	R FT moves BK to 2nd plie	L arm DWN
6	L FT in passe as above	R arm OVRHD as above
7	L FT BK to 2nd, chug FWD by lifting heels	Chest port de bras, BK of palms face FRT in jazz HND.
8	RPT—chug forward	Open to 2nd POS jazz HND on CT 8
1-2	Walk FWD, L, R	Arms at sides
3	Jump to 2nd on plie	HNDS in to SHLS, push strongly with palms to 2nd POS
4	OTR with R heel in passe, flexed FT, TO	Arms cross in FRT of body
5	R FT to 2nd POS in plie	As in CT 3
6-7	Double OTL	As in CT 4
8	Jump to 1st POS in plie, NTO	Arms shoot OVRHD
1	Hold plie	Arms in 1st POS
2	Lunge FWD on R in releve plie, L knee locked	Arms to 4th POS, L FRT
3	Close R FT to L	HNDS in to SHLS
4	L FWD on L as above	Arms to 4th, R FRT
5	Close L FT to R	Arms in to SHLS
6	Lunge BK on R FT, look up	Arms move OVRHD
7	Close R FT to L	Arms DWN to sides
8	Hold FT in 1st POS plie	Hold
1	Step R to 2nd, ISOL L hip	Chest port de bras, BK of jazz HNDS face FRT
2	Cross L in BK of R, FT in demi-plie, L in plie-releve	Hold L HND, R jazz HND moves OVRHD
3	Hold	L SHL moves FWD as R jazz HND stretches BK and DWN (elbows bent)
4	Hold	L SHL moves BK and R SHL FWD, R arm trails, L HND turns palm and moves to 2nd POS

5-8	RPT and REV above 4 CTS to L	RPT and REV above
1&2	Walk FWD R, L and jump to 2nd POS, plie	Palms of HNDS push FWD from SHLS
3	OTR in plie, R knee TO passe	Arms bent OVRHD, jazz HNDS, palms FWD
4	Finish turn in 2nd POS plie	Arms in 2nd POS, palms facing sides
5	Knee roll R	Hold
6	Brush L FT BK to C#4, kicking leg up from knee	Hold
7	Step to 2nd POS on L FT, locked knees	Hold
8	Isolate R knee and CON rib-cage	Chest port de bras
1-8	RPT last 8 CTS, moving BK on CTS 1&2	

Phrase II

1-2	Step R to 2nd in plie, close L to R in 1st POS releve	Arms to 2nd POS jazz HNDS
3	Plie L, PT R toe to 2nd POS	L arm DWN, R HND reaches to high 2nd
4	Step BK on R FT	R HND in to R SHL with clenched fist
5-6	RPT and REV last 2 CTS to L	
7	PT R toe to 2nd	Arms 2nd in jazz HND, palms DWN
8	Step FWD on R FT	Clenched fists in to SHLS
1	Step FWD L to R DIAG to C#1	Arms to 4th POS, L FRT
&2	Kick R FT high from knee 2 Xs. L FT on releve plie	Hold
3	Step on R FT in deep plie	
4	Releve R FT and turn to L facing C#2, battement L leg FWD	Clap HNDS in FRT, elbows locked
5-6	ITL on plie, finish to C#1	
7	Chug FWD with FT in 1st POS NTO, plie	
8	Hold	Both HNDS brush thighs and move BK, HD leans BK
1-16	RPT above last 16 CTS	

Phrase III

1,2,3	Jazz sissonne (plie 5th and jete R to C#1) (R FRT, locked knee, L leg in BK attitude. Land plie R FT.). Step through on L on CT 3.	L arm FRT, R in 2nd
4	R toe PTS in 2nd on FLR, body arches to R over leg	Arms on DIAG, R DWN, L up
5	Tap R toe in BK of L FT	Bend R arm in to chest, BK of palm FRT

6,7,8	Walk R-L-R, circle to R	R opens and passes thru 2nd
&1	Pas de chat L to C#2 (jump to L, develope kick R FRT)	Arms 2nd
2-3	Step R, L to C#2	
4&5&	Double chaine R-L-R-L to C#4	Arms in to chest
6,7,8	Facing FRT, plie L with R in passe, develope kick R to 2nd, step R FWD	Arms reach OVRHD in V POS on kick
1-16	RPT above 16 CTS	
1-2	Step L to 2nd, R knee ISOL, TI and CON rib-cage	Arms in 2nd
3-4	Step R to C#4, tap L BK of R	Arms V POS OVRHD
5-6	RPT CTS 1, 2 above facing S#6	
7-8	Step R, L facing FRT	
1-8	Run in circle to R, reaching as far FWD as possible with each step	OPP arm FWD from FT, HD turns R, L, R, L, etc.
1-8	Step R saute, arabesque L. Step L saute, arabesque R, RPT R and L.	Arms V POS FRT of chest
1&2	Step FWD R to C#2, step L in place, close R to L	Arms in 2nd POS, jazz HNDS
3-4	Step BK L and pivot to face FRT. Close R to L in 1st POS, NTO, releve	Arms at sides
5-6	Step L to C#2, kick R FT low across body	Arms 2nd
&7,8	Step R to 2nd releve, facing FRT. Place L in FRT of R in 5th POS, releve. REL HD on CT 8.	1st
1-8	REV above 8 CTS to C#1	
1-8	Sous-sus (R FRT), demi-plie, CON pelvis, rib-cage and HD	2nd LJA, lift elbows high as torso descends

Hops, Jumps, Leaps

SAUTE ROND DE JAMBE DEVELOPPE

FT 1st POS, locked knees, NTO   Arms 1st POS

COUNTS	BODY MOVEMENT	ARMS
1-2	Run FWD, R-L, plie	Opposition
&3	Large inside RDJ en l'air—saute L	2nd POS LJA
&4	Plie and hop R, developpe kick L to C#2	DIAG (R DWN, L up)
5-8	REV	
1-8	RPT all above	
1-16	RPT again	

DEVELOPPE KICK TO 2nd

STAG LEAP WITH ARABESQUE

STAG ARABESQUE LEAP

PT R toe FWD, 4th POS, locked knees
Arms 4th POS, L FWD

COUNTS	BODY MOVEMENT	ARMS
1-2-3	Walk BK DIAG to C#4, R-L-R	2nd LJA
&	Plie R	Cross FRT chest
4	Stag R arabesque L (R FT to L knee, stag)	V POS OVRHD
5-8	REV to C#3	
1-8	RPT all above	
1-16	RPT above walk FWD	

CHAINE TURNS WITH STAG AND DEVELOPPE KICK

DEVELOPPE KICK—
"PLIE-RELEVE" POSITION

Face S#6   Pt R toe FWD, 4th POS
Arms 4th (L FWD, R 2nd)

COUNTS	BODY MOVEMENT	ARMS
1&2& 3&4&	4 multiple chaine turns FWD R-L-R-L-R-L-R-L	2nd
5	Step R, plie	Cross
&6	Stag FWD R, L BK arabesque	High 4th (L FRT, R 2nd)
&7	DEV kick L FWD, "plie-releve"	2nd
8	Step L FWD	DWN
1-8	RPT above	
1-16	REV and start chaine L	

CHASSE WITH STAG LEAP

LAY-OUT STAG LEAP

R FT BK to C#3   Arms 1st POS

COUNTS	BODY MOVEMENT	ARMS
1&2	Chasse R-L-R to R side	2nd LJA
3-4	Step L BK, R FWD	
5	Plie (preparation for leap), 5th POS	1st POS
&6	Stag leap to R (lay-out FWD to C#1)	4th POS (L FRT)
7-8	Run L-R FWD	
1-8	REV L	
1-16	RPT all above	

BRUSH SAUTE

SAUTE ATTITUDE CONTRACTION

FT 1st POS, locked knees   Arms 1st

COUNTS	BODY MOVEMENT	ARMS
1-2-3	Run R-L-R, plie on 3	2nd, LJA
&4	Brush L FWD, saute R, AST CON torso (L attitude front), land plie R	Jazz HNDS 2nd
5&6& 7&8&	3 multiple chaine turns L, pique turn L CT 8, step R on "&" CT	
1-8	REV and RPT all above	
1-16	RPT R and L	

JETE BATTEMENT LEAP

1st POS NTO   Face S#6   Arms 1st
Travels in large circle R

COUNTS	BODY MOVEMENT	ARMS
1-2	Run R-L to S#5	1st POS
3&4	Grand jete R, brush L thru and battement L FWD and saute R (hop)	2nd POS LJA for jete, 2nd ILJA for battement

BRUSH LEFT AND SAUTE

5-8	RPT and REV jete L (circling to R)	
3, 8's	Keep repeating above R and L	

JETE RIGHT SIDE, BEND RIGHT

1st POS NTO   Face S#6   Arms 1st
Travels in large circle R

COUNTS	BODY MOVEMENT	ARMS
1-2	**Run R-L to S#5**	**1st**
3	**Jete R—torso bends to R side (R leg STR, L leg BK attitude TO)**	**L OVRHD, R 2nd, ILJA**

SIDE STRETCH AND JETE

4	**REV jete L and bend L (L leg STR, R leg BK attitude TO)**	**R OVRHD, L 2nd, ILJA**
5-8	**RPT above R and L**	**Same**
1-8	**RPT above adding multiple chaines to CTS 1&2&, then jete R-L**	**Into chest, then as above**
1-16	**RPT all above (start with runs, then add jetes)**	
1-32	**REV and RPT—start L**	

BATTEMENT AND STAG LEAP COMBINATION

1st POS NTO   Face S#6   Arms 1st

COUNTS	BODY MOVEMENT	ARMS
1-2	**Run R-L to C#1**	**1st POS**
3	**FWD battement R to C#1, saute (hop) L**	**2nd POS ILJA**

BATTEMENT AND SAUTE

&4	**½ turn L (face C#3), FWD battement R, saute L**	**Same**
5-6	**Walk R-L to C#3, torso bends R-L**	**V POS OVRHD**
7	**Plie 5th POS R FRT (still face C#3)**	**1st**
&8	**Stag leap (R FT at L knee, L arabesque, while in air twist torso to C#2)**	**L OVRHD, R 2nd**
1-8	**RPT and REV above run L-R to C#2**	**Same**
1-16	**RPT above R and L**	**Same**

AIR TOUR, BACK ATTITUDE TURN SAUTE

FT 1st PP, locked knees   Arms 1st

COUNTS	BODY MOVEMENT	ARMS
1-2	Run FWD R-L, plie	Lift to 2nd POS, LJA CT 1, 4th POS—R FWD, CT 2
3&	R tour (turn R in air), FT 5th POS	Chest
4	Plie 5th POS, R FRT	1st
&5	Saute and turn R, R leg in BK attitude, L PT to FLR	R OVRHD, L 2nd

SAUTE—RIGHT TURN
RIGHT BACK ATTITUDE

6	Step R FWD	R FWD, L 2nd
&7	ITR—L passe POS, NTO, plie	Chest

INSIDE TURN RIGHT,
L PASSE

8	Lunge L FWD, NTO, plie	2nd ILJA
1-8	RPT all above	Same
1-16	Combination should also be done L	

"When you leave class, you are exhilarated and relaxed."